Versatile Yankee

Versatile Yankee
The Art of Jonathan Fisher, 1768–1847

Alice Winchester

Collector's Imprint Edition
The Pyne Press
Princeton

Library of Congress Catalog Card Number 73-79528

SBN 87861-051-0

Printed by A. Colish, Inc., Mount Vernon, New York

First Edition

116661

Contents

II FLORA

III PAINTINGS IN OIL

List of Works

Sources and Credits

Acknowledgments

In compiling the text of this book I have necessarily relied heavily on Fisher's own records and on the writings of others about the man and his art. With many thanks I acknowledge my debt to the following sources.

Fisher documented his own life and works remarkably well. He habitually though not invariably titled, signed, and dated his pictures, often in a sort of phonetic spelling from which he eventually developed his shorthand. He kept voluminous records of various kinds, and happily his descendants, like himself, have had the admirable New England trait of saving things. Along with many letters, sermons, and notes, the diary that he kept for nearly forty-five years and the *Sketches* of his life composed after 1812—in both of which he frequently mentioned his painting and engraving— have been preserved in Maine; the shorthand in which they are written was deciphered more than a century later by Edith Chase Weren with the assistance of Gaylord C. Hall.

The remarkable history of Jonathan Fisher was told in detail by Mary Ellen Chase, herself a native of Blue Hill, in her colorful biography, *Jonathan Fisher, Maine Parson, 1768-1847*, New York, Macmillan, 1948. Anyone else writing of Fisher must depend on this book, and be grateful for its satisfying completeness. It quotes generously from Fisher's diary and letters, and some of my quotations from them were taken here at second hand.

A brief *Biographical Sketch of the Reverend Jonathan Fisher of Blue Hill, Maine*, by Gaylord C. Hall, a descendant, was privately published in New York, and followed by a *Supplement* in 1946. A letter written in 1855 by the Reverend S. L. Pomroy of Bangor, who knew Fisher for thirty years, was quoted by William Buell Sprague in his *Annals of the American Pulpit*, New York, 1857; I consulted a manuscript copy in the New York Public Library.

An architectural study of Fisher's house was made by Abbott Lowell Cummings in his article "Jonathan Fisher House, Blue Hill, Maine," published in *Old-Time New England*, the bulletin of the Society for the Preservation of New England Antiquities, Vol. LXI, No. 4, 1966.

The first published study of Fisher's artistic production was Janet S. Byrne's "An American Pioneer Amateur," in the *Princeton University Library Chronicle*, Vol. VI, No. 4, June 1945; it identifies most of the published sources for the wood engravings in Fisher's *Scripture Animals* and gives other helpful information. Details about Fisher's engraving and published work are given in Sinclair Hamilton's *Early American Book Illustrators and Wood Engravers 1670-1870*, Princeton, Princeton University Library, 1958. The engravings are briefly discussed in the article "Prints" by Karl Kup in *American Artist*, April 1947.

Hamilton Vaughan Bail's *Views of Harvard; a pictorial record to 1860*, Cambridge, Harvard University Press, 1949, includes a check list of Fisher's Harvard views. Comments on Fisher's painting by Oliver W. Larkin are quoted in Miss Chase's book, and included in briefer form in Larkin's *Art and Life in America*, New York, Holt, Rinehart & Winston, 1960. Fisher as artist is the subject of my article "Rediscovery: Parson Jonathan Fisher" in *Art in America*, Vol. 58, No. 6, November-December 1970, which became my point of departure for this more thorough study.

Fisher's painting was represented in the exhibition *Maine and Its Role in American Art 1740-1963* held at the Museum of Modern Art, New York, in 1963, and in the chapter by Nina Fletcher Little in the book of the same title edited by Elizabeth F. Wilder, New York, Viking, 1963. *The Arts and Crafts of the Versatile Parson Jonathan Fisher 1768-1847* is the useful catalogue of an exhibition held in 1967 at the William A. Farnsworth Library and Art Museum.

For special assistance in the preparation of this book I am very grateful to William P. Hinckley, president of the Jonathan Fisher Memorial, Inc.; Wendell S. Hadlock, director of the William A. Farnsworth Library and Art Museum; Robert S. Fraser, curator of rare books, Princeton University Library; Prof. Henry S. Horn, Department of Biology, Princeton University; Pauline W. Inman, Jean Lipman, former editor of *Art in America*; and Mary M. Meehan of the Harvard University Archives.

Introduction

At the age of fifty-six the Reverend Jonathan Fisher sat before a looking glass in his house in Blue Hill, Maine, and painted a picture of himself. It shows him keen-eyed, deeply wrinkled, and intense, seated at a table with his finger on an open copy of the Bible in Hebrew. Beside the book, with his inkwell and quill, are a folded letter and a scrap of paper clearly inscribed with his name and address, his age, and the date. Fisher recorded in his diary that he painted his portrait between April 19 and April 28, 1824, and that it was "not so good as I should have wished." Soon afterward he made a second attempt, a direct copy of the first. Then nearly fifteen years later he made two more, so that each of his daughters might have one.

By profession Fisher was a clergyman, not an artist. For forty-one years he was minister of the Congregational Church at Blue Hill. But all his life he made pictures, and that was only one of his avo-cations and accomplishments. Inventor, architect and builder, surveyor, linguist, naturalist, teacher, poet—Jonathan Fisher was all these and more. A contemporary said that his minutes were as precious to him as money to a miser, and indeed he must never have lost or misspent one.

He was a great reader, and had a remarkable library for one in his isolated location and pecuniary straits. He mastered Hebrew, Greek, Latin, and French, and had some knowledge of Arabic, Malay, and the Penobscot Indian language. He invented a shorthand code that he called his "philosophical alphabet," which he claimed saved him seventy dollars in paper during his lifetime because he wrote all his sermons and copies of all his letters in it, as well as the diary that he kept for nearly forty-five years. He compiled a Hebrew lexicon. He made surveying instruments, and with them laid out roads in Blue Hill and mapped the region. He built his own house

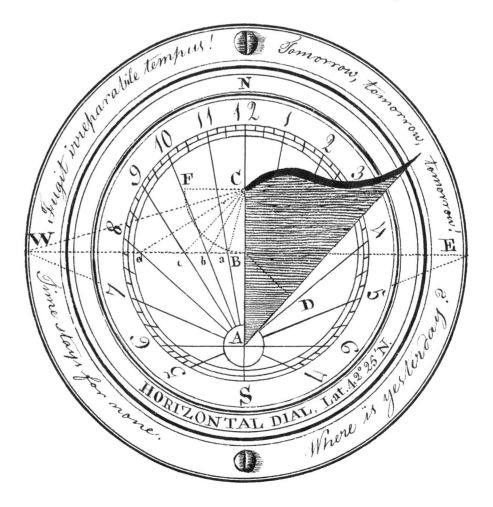

and made his furniture. His study table was convertible into a work bench, so that, as a friend said, he could in a moment pass from head work to handiwork. He made and mended furniture for his neighbors as well, and made and painted sleighs and carriages. To eke out his meager income he made and sold an extraordinary variety of useful objects, from buttons and straw braid to pumps and picture frames. Of necessity he was a farmer, raising crops and livestock to feed his family, and he made his own farm implements and household utensils.

Of all his activities, Fisher found his art one of the most congenial. He wrote that during his college days his "principal instruments of relaxation" were "the pen, the pencil, and the tools of the mechanic," and throughout his life he took greatest pleasure in making pictures, writing verse, and fashioning things with his hands. His *oeuvre*, if that is not too formal a word for it, consists of drawings in ink, paintings in water color and in oil, and engravings on wood. They show him to have been uncommonly gifted and exceptionally prolific and versatile. In spite of an evident lack of technical proficiency, they reveal a direct approach and spontaneous vitality, impelled by an enthusiasm for subjects chosen from nature and a striving for simple realism.

Most of Fisher's pictures are preserved in two important collections, one in his house at Blue Hill, now the Jonathan Fisher Memorial, Inc., the other at the William A. Farnsworth Library and Art Museum in Rockland, Maine. These comprise the majority of his known paintings, his notebooks and albums of water colors, his paint box, many wood engravings that he printed himself and copies of books he illustrated, some of his wood blocks with the drawings he made for them, and his engraving tools—besides a great variety of other things he made and used.

Fisher lived in obscurity and remains today a minor figure in the history of American art but he is not unknown and he has ardent admirers. As interest in him has gradually increased during the past twenty-five years or so, some of his pictures have been shown in exhibitions and discussed and illustrated in publications, but the full scope of his work has not yet been presented. That is the aim of this book.

This introductory study is an attempt to survey Fisher's complete artistic production, trace its chronological development, and classify it in terms of medium and date. With this approach, new discoveries have been made about his methods of work and the pattern of his progress which are brought out in the text, and unrecorded examples of his painting have been found which are included in the appended list of his works.

The major portion of the book is devoted to illustrating Fisher's work itself. Most of his paintings are published here, and for the first time: the majority of water colors from his notebooks, reproduced in color and in approximately actual size, along with a selection of his most important paintings in oil. A representative selection of his wood engravings is also included.

Jonathan Fisher was born October 7, 1768, at New Braintree in central Massachusetts, the eldest son of Jonathan and Katharine Avery Fisher. His parents moved westward in 1773 to Northampton, where the senior Fisher built a one-room log "cottage" for his growing family. In 1776 he joined up as a second lieutenant to fight in the Revolution, and only a year later he died, of a fever. Katharine Fisher, an impecunious widow at the age of thirty-nine, had to break up housekeeping and distribute her seven children among relatives. Jonathan, nine years old, was "put to live" with his uncle Joseph Avery, minister of the Congregational Church at Holden, Massachusetts, and there he stayed until he was nearly twenty.

While most of his time was occupied in doing chores around the house and on the farm, his uncle gave him lessons in Latin, Greek, and theology, and for a few weeks each year Jonathan went to school. He had a lively mind and was encouraged to use it, particularly by his mother, who was well-read herself and was ambitious for him to become a minister. That meant going to college, poor as the family was, and in 1788, after two or three years of studying "in great earnestness," Jonathan was admitted to Harvard. To help pay his way he obtained a "waitership" in the commons, worked in the library, taught school, and made things he could sell. He graduated in 1792 and spent another three years at Harvard as a divinity student to win his Master of Arts degree.

During the summers of 1794 and 1795 Fisher served the Congregational Church at Blue Hill, and in 1796 he became its first permanent pastor—indeed, the first settled minister east of the Penobscot River. Blue Hill, a fishing and farming village clinging to the remote rocky coast of Maine, had been incorporated as a town only seven years before. The whole surrounding region of "Unappropriated Wilderness and Islands" had been opened to settlement for little more than thirty years, and except for a few scattered villages it was still a wilderness. The people of Blue Hill had built a grist mill, sawmills, docks, and some substantial houses, and cleared enough land for farms and pastures. In 1792 they raised the meetinghouse and the following summer

finished it outside, though work on the interior went on for several years. Fisher himself painted and numbered the pews in 1799. Maine was a district of Massachusetts until it became a state in 1820, and Boston, two or three days distant from Blue Hill by boat, was more accessible than inland settlements. Even by 1824, when Fisher painted a picture of Blue Hill, it was still a straggling village tucked in between ocean and virgin forest.

In November 1796 Fisher took his bride to Blue Hill. She was Dolly Battle of Dedham, the town near Boston where Fisher's forebears had lived since the mid-1600's and where he spent his vacations with relatives. Just a year later the couple moved into the house he had built on the cleared lot provided as part of his compensation, which also included fifteen cords of hardwood, a new barn, and a salary of $200 a year. That house in time became the ell of a larger house that Fisher added to it in 1814. This he planned with greatest care and considerable originality, and characteristically he kept a complete record of his designs and of the progress of

construction, illustrating it with drawings of floor plan, framing, sash, doors, and wainscoting. In 1896 the ell—that is, the original house—was torn down and replaced with a new one, but the 1814 structure still stands as Fisher built it. Today it is a registered historic landmark, maintained by the Jonathan Fisher Memorial, Inc., which was founded in 1954.

In this small parsonage Fisher and his wife raised a family of nine children, which was frequently augmented by young men who boarded with them while training under Fisher's tutelage for the ministry. "The walls of his dwelling," a fellow clergyman wrote, "were ornamented with paintings, the work of his own hands"—as was the dwelling itself. It is a simple, two-story, hip-roofed house, painted yellow outside with ocher from Fisher's farm, sheathed inside in unpainted pine, and it has one large and one small room and a stair hall on each floor. The smaller ground-floor room, with two windows and a fireplace, was the parson's study, and here his chest of tools stood beside his study table. One of his

daughters told her friend Sarah Perry that "when she was pestered by the other children she took refuge in this sanctum," and while she sat on the tool chest "her father taught her botany and talked to her in French."

In proportions and general appearance the house represents the Federal style of the period when Fisher built it, though some of its exterior details suggest the Greek Revival that had hardly yet come into popularity, while the interior recalls many older New England farmhouses. It has some ingenious features, such as a partition between two rooms which bisects a window, a central chimney that is actually off-center, and a built-in clock. That clock was a typical Fisher creation. While he was spending a spring vacation in Dedham in 1790 he noted in his diary, "Began a wooden clock," and regularly from then on he worked on it during vacations until finally, on July 22, 1792, he was able to record, "Finished the inner structure of my clock & set it a going." Then he made and stained the clock case. Twenty-five years later, in 1817, he moved the clock

to Blue Hill and installed it in the woodwork of his house, where it ran for another fifty years. He painted a new dial for it, on paper fixed to cardboard, which he signed and dated and inscribed with mottoes in Hebrew, Greek, Latin, French, and in English, "Beholder, thou art NOW alive." He also added an alarm mechanism that would ring between the hours of three and six—evidently not needing it for any later hour of the morning. According to one of his daughters, Fisher rose every day at five o'clock, wakened by this alarm, and "read a chapter in the Hebrew Bible aloud, to keep his ear correct, and at family worship read from a French Bible."

Fisher had begun learning French while he was at Cambridge and soon was reading Pascal, who became his favorite writer. He admired the French theologian both for his literary style and for his religious views which, though Catholic, were closely akin to his own Calvinist belief in predestination and salvation by divine grace. Throughout his life he continued to read religious and theological writings in both English and French, and to enjoy the Latin and Greek classics he had read in college, as well as the English poets and philosophers of the seventeenth and eighteenth centuries.

For over forty years Fisher fulfilled his ministerial duties with dedication and zeal, so faithfully indeed that it seems miraculous that he found time for all the other things he did. He preached twice on Sunday and once on Thursday and held monthly prayer meetings; he wrote and delivered literally thousands of sermons. In addition he gave frequent lectures on religious and philosophical subjects and conducted meetings of missionary and other societies, taught the children of the town and catechized them rigorously, visited the sick and troubled, officiated at baptisms, marriages, and funerals and kept a record of all births and deaths, and joined in all the events and activities that made up the life of his isolated community. Convinced of the necessity for education, he was instrumental in the founding in 1803 of Blue Hill Academy, one of the earliest schools in Maine, and was president of its board of trustees for many years; it is significant that he favored including painting and music as well as the

classics and mathematics in the curriculum. He was also a founder of the school that became the Bangor Theological Seminary and for many years served as a trustee.

While his own congregation was small he extended his ministry, meeting and working with pastors of other churches in the county and serving as a missionary to outlying villages far in the wilderness. He traveled many miles within his own parish, and many more outside it—all on foot. Summer and winter and through mud time in the spring he would walk the seventy miles to Bangor and back, and comparable distances "through the forest" to other settlements. On his first missionary journey to communities farther east, in 1801, he walked three hundred miles in one month. On a long trek through a snowstorm he composed one of his poems:

> Traveling still westward, as I pass along,
> The tempest, rushing with unbridled force,
> Beats full upon me; piercing is the cold;
> I turn my face a little to the left,
> Hold my right hand against the windward cheek,
> And thus defend it from the beating snow.
> Sometimes I wade through drifts; anon the path,
> Clear'd by the wind, affords a better way
> To trip it lightly. Thus I journey on;
> The knee, some weary, gives a little pain;
> But all is well. The busy mind within,
> Calm and unruffled, smiling at the storm,
> Surveys a thousand beauties.

Fisher's spiritual influence was great among several generations of people living in Blue Hill and far beyond. He preached and practiced an uncompromising Calvinism, sternly combating the rising influence of Arminianism and other doctrines he felt to be false. He strongly opposed slavery and war and violence of every kind. He gave active support to the temperance movement, the colonization of Liberia, and efforts to improve the condition of American Indians. He shared his learning and his intellectual interests, broadening the horizons of his remote village and contributing in every way to its cultural dignity.

Jonathan Fisher is said by some to have been solemn and rather forbidding, with little sense of humor, though one who knew him described him as a happy man, pious and without guile, always cheerful, and "ever what he seemed to be." Obviously he took himself seriously, but his strong convictions about right and wrong, his lively curiosity about many things, and his evident enthusiasms must have made him a vital and stimulating personality. Certainly from this distance he is a fascinating figure. In 1837 he retired as pastor of the church at Blue Hill, and he died there in his seventy-ninth year on September 22, 1847.

It was during his years at Harvard, especially the postgraduate years, that Jonathan Fisher cultivated his interest in making pictures, though as he himself said he had laid the groundwork for it in his boyhood. In the *Sketches* of his life which he began compiling in his forties he wrote, "Between the years of 10 and 15 of my age I began to exhibit some traces of a mechanical genius and a turn toward mathematics, spending my leisure time in making buttons, brooches, windmills, snares, traps, purling sticks, and the like, and in solving various questions in mathematics, sometimes with a pin on a smooth board and sometimes on a slate, which led the way afterwards to a small measure of proficiency in sketching and painting."

Apparently he received no instruction in art beyond the mechanical drawing required for geometry, surveying, and related courses at Harvard. His studies there were concentrated mainly in Latin, Greek, and Hebrew, English grammar and literature, mathematics (which he found "particularly pleasing"), philosophy, theology, and natural philosophy, or what may be called the physical sciences. Nevertheless, the accounts which he kept meticulously to the penny show that aside from payments for textbooks his major expenditures were for paper and art materials—such items as India ink and Dutch quills, carmine, vermilion, umber, English ocher, and white lead. And the drawings and paintings that he made and carefully signed and dated between 1791 and 1795 make up the greater part, quantitatively, of those that are known today. At that time, too, he began to experiment with engraving on wood, a technique which he was to put to good use thirty years later.

As part of his college work Fisher made a "Perspective View" of Harvard's Hollis Hall, which is now preserved in the Harvard Archives with other "mathematical theses" required of students from 1782 to 1839. The view itself is a water-color sketch of Hollis and nearby buildings framed in an oval, but that was only part of the exercise. The rest of the large sheet on which it appears is filled with "orthographical projections," or architectural working plans, of the front and end of the building, neatly measured, drawn, and lettered; and in the lower right corner, wreathed in a floral spray, is an inscription: "To the Governors of Harvard College .

. . . Humbly Presented by their dutiful Pupil, Jonathan Fisher, September 27th. 1791."

This was among the first of many views of Harvard that Fisher painted. In 1949 Hamilton Vaughan Bail recorded eleven, of which two were unlocated. Now fourteen are known, eleven in water color and three in oil, and he evidently produced still more. Most of those in water color are signed and dated in 1793, 1794, and 1795. As early as September 1790 Fisher wrote in his diary, "Sketched and painted a view of the Colleges," and in May 1791, "Finished painting a view from my study window"—a view which probably showed college buildings since he lived in Massachusetts Hall —but these two pictures antedating the perspective

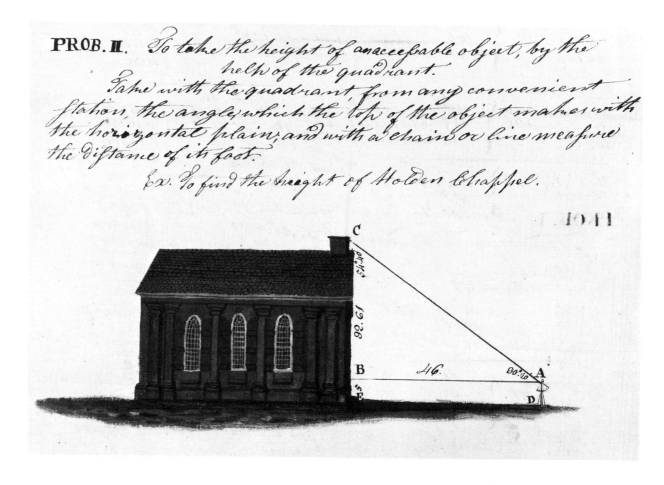

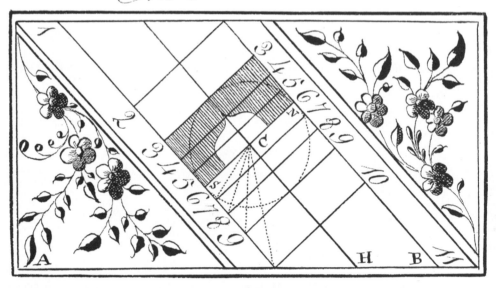

An East Dial.

view of September 1791 are not known to exist today. A view of Hollis, Harvard, and Massachusetts Halls dated 1794 is inscribed "No. 6," though only two earlier views are now known. That 1794 view has a curious and ingenious feature: the many small windowpanes within their painted white frames are punched full of pinholes, in the manner of the "pin-pricked pictures" made at the time by schoolgirls and other amateurs.

All these water colors of Harvard have an appealing naïveté. The buildings are drawn with a painstaking accuracy that gives them historical value, and the few cows and human figures in the foregrounds add interest and life. The colors are opaque and Bail identified them as *gouache*.

Besides these views, Fisher began to paint during his college years small water-color sketches of a variety of subjects. In most of them the color is opaque, sometimes even dull and muddy, only occasionally brilliant. Some are amusingly inept, some are vividly realistic. Together they make up a distinctive, colorful, and thoroughly engaging body of his work.

More than a hundred of these pictures are preserved in volumes which Fisher himself bound in leather. One notebook, which he titled *Mathematics,* contains some of his earliest artistic efforts and demonstrates that progression from solving mathematical problems to sketching and painting which he had observed in himself. It consists of college work from 1791 to 1793, giving solutions to problems in geometry, trigonometry, surveying, and navigation. The diagrams are carefully drawn and lettered in black and red ink, and many are illuminated with "flowers and sprigs" in water color. A rosy apple with red blossoms that look like carnations growing from the same stem adorns *The Plain Scale,* and a spray of multicolored carnations takes up most of the page headed "Elements of Geometry." The book's title is lettered within a border of flowers, and mottoes in Latin and Greek at the beginning and end are embellished by calligraphic scrolls. A full page is devoted to an "Apology for Mathematics, 1791" that expresses Fisher's dual appreciation of the sciences and the arts:

THE BOAR.

THE WILD BOAR.

Some court the muse to lend the harmonious strain,
Cull the sweet flowers from every blooming plain.
Some for their thoughts prefer a different dress,
And free in prose their sentiments express.
These choose to soar unfetter'd, unconfin'd,
Those in soft chains their willing numbers bind.
Some guide the pencil, charm our wond'ring eyes;
Bid the fair landscape rich in beauty rise;
To lifeless matter animation give;
By art illusive make the canvas live.
Some with sweet sounds enchant the listening ear,
Calm rage to rest, and stop the rising tear.
Orpheus! 'twas thine; and Handel! thine to warm
The captive breast, the fetter'd soul to charm.
　　These noble minds obtain a deathless name,
Are led by genius to immortal fame.
Nor these alone; great Newton! thou shalt stand
High in the rolls of every age and land;
Euclid was thine; o'er him 'twas thine to rise
From measuring earth to mete the expanded skies.

Another notebook consists almost entirely of water-color sketches of animals, birds, flowers, fruits, and insects. Many pages are headed "Natural History" and a number are dated 1793 and 1794; others, dated from 1800 to 1826, were probably painted after Fisher had gathered and bound the sheets preserved from his college days.

A smaller notebook with the title *Varietas* has endpapers signed in elaborate calligraphy with Fisher's name and the dates 1790 and 1814. Scattered through, under a variety of headings, are sketches of animals, birds, and insects, and quotations from books, including "Receipts for those who paint in water colors" and "Recipes. To secure Cabbage plants from worms. To make bad butter good. For a weeping sinew."

The largest of Fisher's volumes is a sketchbook in full folio size, with the title, lettered in the phonetic spelling which was an early form of his shorthand, *A Collection of Natural History*. It contains some thirty water colors of animals, birds, plants, and shells, dated in 1795, 1810, 1840, and 1841. Half a dozen were drawn "from nature"; the rest were copied from illustrations in books. Twenty were copied from *Gleanings of Natural History, exhibiting figures of quadrupeds, birds, insects, plants, &c. ...* by George Edwards (1694-1773). The three volumes under this title, published in London between 1758 and 1764, complete Edwards' seven-

THE HOG of SIAM.

The young wild Boar.

The sucking pig.

volume *Natural History*. Fisher inscribed the English naturalist's name and that of his book on his pictures, usually along with his own name and the date, and in most cases he also gave in full the descriptive text which was printed below Edwards' illustrations in two parallel columns, one in English, the other in French. He deviated from the original only in the English text, which he transcribed in his shorthand. His water colors are meticulously copied from Edwards' hand-colored engravings, even to the script lettering close to the picture on many of the plates. Fisher's colors are not so clear as Edwards', however, his shading is rather less crisp, and sometimes his drawing reveals a certain constraint.

At Harvard Fisher wrote repeatedly in his diary of "drawing from the library" books on science and theology and "several having to do with Natural History." According to the College Laws "certain books of great value" could be borrowed only by special permission, and the College Records in the Harvard Archives state that on May 20, 1795, at a meeting of the president and fellows of the college it was "voted that Sir Fisher be permitted to take *Edward's Gleanings* from the Library." Later Fisher himself owned a copy of this precious book. His interest in botany and in zoology in all its branches was paramount and lasting. As early as 1791 he conceived the idea of writing and illustrating a book on natural history, and though he never completed it in the form originally planned, he continued to make his sketches of flora and fauna for most of his life.

The creatures he depicted make an odd assortment. Most of the animals and birds are native to Africa and other distant parts that Fisher never saw —rhinoceros, elephant, hyena, zebra, crowned eagle, monkey, macaw—while the larkspur and garden pea, apples and pears, spider and bees that he painted were commonplace in his own New England. Obviously the exotic fauna were copied, and Fisher named several sources besides Edwards. The rhinoceros and hyena are "from Bruce's Travels"; James Bruce's *Travels to Discover the Source of the Nile* was published in Dublin in 1790. Fisher's page of shellfish is "from Hill's Natural History"; the

This view of the Catamount was drawn from one in the possession of Gen. Washington &c.

Drawn and painted by J. Fisher
June 19th 17..

third volume of *A General Natural History* by John Hill, published in London in 1752, is devoted to animals, birds, fishes, and insects. The crow, though hardly unfamiliar to Fisher, he took "from Buffon," the great French naturalist whose *Histoire naturelle* was the first comprehensive presentation in popular form of the various branches of natural history. Its forty-four volumes were published in Paris between 1749 and 1804, and the Harvard library early acquired those on birds and quadrupeds.

The lion was one exotic beast that Fisher could and did portray from life. He noted in his diary that he went to Boston and paid fifty cents to see a live lion that had been brought from Africa, and on his picture of it he wrote, "Drawn from nature, and painted Feb. 20, 1795." He made two pictures of the catamount, both from life—though not startlingly lifelike. The first he dated June 17, 1793, and his account book for that year shows that he spent 12½ cents for "several sights at a live catamount." The second drawing, dated in the 1790's (the last digit is trimmed off), shows a powerful beast brought in infancy from the Ohio country, as he wrote below it. Despite its bared teeth and straining stance, it looks rather like a friendly cat.

Altogether these water-color sketches of Fisher's make a brilliant menagerie. Some of the pictures of creatures he had never seen show a faulty under-

standing of their anatomy, some are awkwardly drawn, some are more stylized than realistic, but almost all are lively and colorful and reveal the eager enthusiasm of their painter.

Fisher consulted at least one of the drawing books that had been available in England since the early 1600's and had begun to be published in the United States before 1790. These art-instruction books usually included illustrations for aspirant artists to copy and were full of useful information on how to make pictures in various mediums—sometimes the same information repeated verbatim from book to book. The "Receipts for those who paint in water colors" that Fisher copied in his *Varietas* album list ways

To make gum water.
Another way.
To keep flies from your work.
To make liquid gold for vellum painting.
To make liquid silver for the same.
To make the glare of eggs.
To recover liquid silver, that has contracted rust.
To keep colors from sinking.
To make size for painting scenes & other candle light pieces.
To recover colors, when decayed.

These very instructions are given in a little book called *The Artists Assistant in Drawing, Perspective, Etching, Engraving, Mezzotinto-scraping, Painting on Glass, in Crayons, and in Water-Col-*

ours, which was first published in London about 1760 and reappeared again and again in "improved" editions. Fisher must have seen or even owned a copy.

Many of the plates published in the drawing books were of the human figure, which seems not to have attracted Fisher though he drew one page of eyes; but there were many, too, of flowers and animals, buildings, landscapes, and studies in perspective. He could easily have found models for the flowers and sprigs that he strewed over his sheets.

While most of the water colors that Fisher copied from printed sources were done, as it now appears, during his college years, most of those that he labeled "drawn from life" or "from nature" or "drawn to the full size" are shown by their dates and often by specific inscriptions to have been painted after he moved to Maine. On his "Common, full grown Grasshopper, taken from the life, in Bluehill, Maine, August 18, 1826," he added the comment, "This year grasshoppers in the State of Maine were exceedingly numerous." His picture of the carrot, a real natural wonder, is fully documented in script and fancy lettering: "A careful imitation of a CARROT raised in Bluehill, in the year 1807, in the garden of the Rev. Jonathan Fisher./The curious braid of the CARROT was formed by nature, without any interposition of human art. Attest, Jonathan

Fisher, Bluehill, January 29, 1808./Drawn and painted by candle light Jan 28, 1808, by Jon. Fisher, Bluehill."

A telling little still life of two apples on a pewter plate, though undated, was very likely painted at Blue Hill. One readily visualizes Fisher picking the fruit from one of his trees and putting it on the home-made pine table in the parsonage kitchen. Oliver W. Larkin wrote of this picture, "At a time when few American artists practised still life painting, Fisher made his exquisite small watercolor of apples on a pewter plate, rounding them off with patient gradations and setting them firmly in space."

Perhaps the most appealing of all the water colors in Fisher's albums shows a big black horse against a little view framed in an oval. The glossy saddled horse prances along the road beside fenced fields; a lane at the left leads to a red and a yellow house, and rounded hills rise in the far distance. Highlights on the saddle and houses and clouds are accented in gilt. The landscape is painted rather sketchily, but the horse is portrayed with care and with spirit, as an important personage. The view is clearly of Blue Hill, and Fisher inscribed it there, though on the date he gave, December 30, 1800, the village would have been buried in snow, not green with grass and leaves as he painted it. He lettered a verse from the Book of Job below the scene: "Hast thou given the

HORSE strength?" Fisher did not have a horse of his own until twenty-four years later.

It was at Blue Hill, evidently, that Fisher produced his paintings in oil on canvas and on panel. Twenty-two of these are known, all in frames that he made himself. Like his water colors, they include copies from prints, but the majority are original works. Seven are undated; dates on the others range from 1807 to 1847, the year of his death. The subjects vary from portraits and views to still life, religious and literary themes, and nature studies, and the sizes from less than 12 by 10 inches to nearly 27 by 60. The paintings vary in quality as well. The most successful, and the most numerous, are those done in the 1820's and 1830's. In the two dated 1847 one can sense the effect of his failing eyesight; in 1841 he had written his children, "My sight, hearing, and memory are all waning."

Fisher painted in oil three views of Harvard College buildings, similar in composition to some of his water-color views of the 1790's and probably copied from them. All are unsigned and undated, though one has been inscribed by another hand than his, "Parson Fisher 1790." Most probably that date is erroneous. It seems unlikely that Fisher would have attempted this fairly complex composition in oil earlier than any of his water-color sketches of Harvard. Indeed, so far as can be determined, he had not even begun to paint in oil in 1790. While his journals and accounts suggest that he was experimenting with it during his later years at Harvard, none of his work in oil can be confidently ascribed to a date earlier than 1798. In that year he recorded painting a view of Dedham, and though as usual he did not identify the medium, more than one oil of Dedham exists while no water color of the town is known.

One other college view in oil by Fisher is known —not of Harvard but of Nassau Hall and the President's House at Princeton. It is signed and dated "Feb. 1807" and inscribed "from an old print." The source was a copperplate engraving by Henry Dawkins, published in 1764 as an illustration of the book *A True Account of the College of New Jersey*. In his diary Fisher wrote of working on it in late 1806 and early 1807, and in February he "Finished landscape and frame for Esquire Peters. Price 12 dollars." The purchaser has been identified by Janet S. Byrne as John Peters, a leading citizen of Blue Hill and a neighbor of Fisher's, but no connection with Princeton on the part of either patron or painter that would explain why the subject was chosen has been discovered. Perhaps it was simply because the "old print" happened to be owned by someone in Blue Hill and Esquire Peters fancied it.

Translating the uncolored engraving into an oil painting required major adjustments on Fisher's part. The print measured 9¾ by 14¾ inches, and he filled a canvas of different proportions and much greater size, 26½ by 59½ inches. Moreover, he had to imagine the colors, and quite logically he made the stone of Nassau Hall look like the familiar gray granite of New England, whereas it is actually a New Jersey sandstone of a warm tawny tone. And in the distance he sketched hilly contours not unlike those he knew at Blue Hill, though there are no hills around Princeton. If Fisher had ever seen the New Jersey college he could not have painted it just as he did; yet his depiction of the two buildings repeats all the architectural detail recorded in the print, and, like Fisher's Harvard views, it is attractive and historically valuable.

Two religious subjects among Fisher's oils, *Descent from the Cross*, undated, and *Gethsemane*, 1838, are also copied from prints. The latter he inscribed "From a print engraved by W. Fathorne, Enlarged & Painted by J. Fisher." The source of the other has not been identified. Possibly both were illustrations in one of his Bibles. At Harvard he had admired some "elegant cuts" in a French Bible in the library, and he wrote there of painting pictures of Adam and Eve and of David and Goliath.

A large undated picture of *Paul and Virginia* may have been based on a book illustration, or, as the character of the design suggests, it may have been copied from a scenic wallpaper of the type that became popular in the 1820's. A painting of a mongoose, the smallest of the oils, Fisher copied from a water color of his own, which in turn he had copied from George Edwards.

An oil dated May 1822 shows a girl in a saffron gown with rosebuds in her hair, seated at a table on which are a rose and an inkwell holding quills; it is captioned *Spring*, with a verse. According to family tradition this is a portrait of one of Fisher's daughters, and so it may be, though Fisher himself indicated that it was after an eighteenth-century French print: to his customary signature he added the words "from Lemire." The work of the French engraver Noël Le Mire (1724-1801) included many book illustrations, some of them allegorical subjects and portraits. While Fisher evidently based this composition on one of Le Mire's prints, it is perhaps not so exact a copy as he usually made. He introduced his own inkwell—surely the very one he showed later in his self-portrait—and the table in the foreground, which cuts rather awkwardly across the figure, may be the one in his study. So the face of *Spring* may indeed be that of his daughter. The verse inscribed on the painting conveys in its few lines all the pious hope and the love of growing things that are characteristic of Fisher:

> Youth is the Spring, when those celestial flowers
> Shou'd bud and Blossom in the cultur'd mind,
> Which give to life a Summer free from blight,
> And yield an Autumn rich in holy fruit,
> Matur'd, and waiting joyful harvest home.

More numerous than the oils Fisher copied, and on the whole more interesting, are his original paintings. Even when they reveal his technical shortcomings they have an endearing personal quality, and some of them represent his best work. A colorful oil "Drawn from nature" in October 1820 portrays four birds native to Maine which Fisher composed in a habitat setting. A still life shows a heap of squashes, ears of corn, and apples that doubtless came from Fisher's farm; it is signed and dated 1832, titled *The Latter Harvest*, and thankfully inscribed with a verse from Psalm 65, "Thou crownest the year with thy goodness." In his picture of a recumbent cow in a pasture Fisher devoted a whole canvas to a figure which was rather a favorite of his—he frequently placed cows in the foreground of his Harvard views and other scenes—but it must be admitted that this portrait, probably of a cow he owned and loved, is not outstandingly successful.

The most important of Fisher's oils are his self-portrait in its four versions and his view of Blue Hill. The portrait shows the parson at home in the study where he wrote his sermons and letters, kept his journal and his accounts, worked on his ingenious inventions, taught and amused his children, and painted his pictures. This very personal portrayal is artistically more confident and accomplished than any of his other works. As Larkin wrote, "When Fisher limned his own portrait, he revealed the whole man. This is not the customary 'primitive' likeness, so often a flat, maplike presentation. The shading of the head gives it a startling and solid reality against the dark background; and on this firm structure Fisher has traced every wrinkle and crease which age and character produce. One can believe that these eyes missed nothing in the world around him; that this strong hand could carve wood and metal; that this forefinger could stab the consciences of his parishioners."

All four paintings have great vigor and honesty and real power, although they are not identical. In the later versions those marks of age and character are more pronounced than in what is apparently the first one, the eyes are more brilliant, and the face is correspondingly more arresting. The panels of the door in the right background are more clearly delineated in the first version, providing a balance to the coat that hangs on the left in the manner of a classical drapery. The pictures differ slightly in size, and the inscriptions vary too. In two portraits the paper at the right is inscribed "Jon. Fisher pinx. Aetatis 56 1824," and in the later ones, "Jon. Fisher pinx. 1824 Aetatis 56 Transcr. 1838." Again, in the earliest version the letter at the left shows the figure "25" written in the corner to indicate postage paid, while in the others the postage is "18½," written in red, and there is a red cancellation stamp with the address "Paterson, N. Jersey" and the date "Feb. 16." Fisher's brother Samuel, also a minister, had settled in Paterson.

Fisher's vivid portrait of himself has been supplemented by the word picture of a contemporary, the Reverend S. L. Pomroy of Bangor: "In personal appearance he was somewhat peculiar, being in stature rather below the middle height, dressed in the antique style, with small clothes, knee buckles & shoes & long waisted ancient coat; his head and neck thrown slightly forward, his head bald & his whole appearance & demeanor unmistakably clerical & grave."

Six months after painting his first self-portrait, Fisher painted and signed *A morning View of Blue-hill / Village. Sept. 1824 / Jon. Fisher pinx*. It is a large horizontal picture, which he framed in a simple pine molding painted black. In 1847 he wrote that he had made a copy of his "view of Blue-hill for Mrs. Cole," but no other version of this charming scene is known to exist today.

The view is full of fascinating detail and as an accurate delineation of an early nineteenth-century Maine seacoast village is a valuable document. Fisher painted his parish just as he saw it—his church and his own house and barn, the houses and farms of his neighbors, the harbor with a full-rigged vessel on the water and three partially built boats on the shore, the green pastures neatly marked off with stump and painted wooden fences and a long stone wall, the forest not far beyond where leaves were taking on their autumn colors, and in the distance the blue hill which gave the town its name. Two women in sunbonnets and a horse are posed in the foreground, while a man with stick raised to strike a long black snake provides a bit of dramatic action.

Fisher also painted in oil three views of Dedham, depicting the homes of friends and relatives in the town where he spent many happy weeks from year to year. An undated view which has traditionally been said to have been done about 1790 may well be the one that, according to his diary, he painted in April 1798. An untitled, undated view of a house and landscape is believed by a descendant to show the Avery house in Dedham, home of Fisher's mother's family. He wrote in his journal that he painted that house in June 1803. Another Dedham picture, dated 1822, shows the handsome large house and barn of Pliny Bingham, surrounded by white fences and stone walls, with church and houses in the distance and three cows in the foreground. These views reveal the same kind of personal vision as Fisher's other original works, and have the historical interest if not the large size and panoramic character of his Blue Hill view.

Fisher's first allusion to engraving, in his journals, was in July 1793, when he was spending a college vacation at Dedham: "Worked on the farm; engraved on boxwood, began a small printing press." A few days later he "Worked on printing press and haying," and early in August "Worked some on the farm. Finished my printing press; engraved a little and struck off a number of prints from boxwood cuts."

Three years later he turned this new technique to commercial use. He was in Dedham, about to be married, and between October 25 and 28 he "Prepared boxwood and engraved a headpiece for the Minerva, [a newspaper] printed at Dedham. . . . Finished my cut and gave it to the printer." Then, actually on his wedding day, November 2, 1796, "Worked a.m. on a cut for the printers and received of them the life of Thomas Paine."

In April 1807 Fisher began work on a book which he continued "in leisure moments" for eight years. In 1811, for example, he noted in his diary, "Writing Youth's Primer and engraving cuts for it." In 1817 the book, "Adorned with cuts," was published by Samuel T. Armstrong of Boston. The lengthy title describes it: *The Youth's Primer, con-*

taining a series of short verses in alphabetical order, each followed by religious, moral or historical observations . . . It is illustrated with twenty-eight wood engravings, most of them signed with Fisher's name or initials, and dated between 1807 and 1812. According to the title page, this book was "designed to be a Sequel to the Child's Primer," and indeed it is closely patterned after the little book generally known as the New England Primer from which generations of children learned their ABC's.

During the next ten years engravings by Fisher illustrated *Hymns for Infant Minds,* published in Boston in 1819, and two other hymnbooks for children; *Youthful Piety: A Memoir . . .,* Boston, 1820; and his own *Short Poems: including a Sketch of the Scriptures . . .,* published in Portland, Maine, in 1827. He also illustrated a couple of broadsides and produced numerous bookplates and other small cuts.

Finally in 1834, when he was sixty-six years old, Fisher's magnum opus appeared. Like his other books, in the fashion of the time, it has a long descriptive title: *Scripture Animals, or Natural History of the Living Creatures named in the Bible, Written Especially for Youth.* He had worked on it for nearly fifteen years, and eventually succeeded in finding a publisher in William Hyde of Portland, who brought out an edition of a thousand copies, of which Fisher bought 625 and peddled them himself.

In this curious and quite fascinating little volume Fisher's lifetime passion for nature and art came together with his intimate knowledge of the Bible and his concern for religious training of the young. The book on natural history that he had envisioned in his college days never materialized but his variation on the theme served to satisfy other interests of his as well. Its didactic purpose is clearly stated in his introductory note: "The work is designed especially to assist young people in gaining a knowledge of the natural history of the Bible. . . . At the close of most of the articles I have added something in the way of moralizing. . . ."

For the title page of the book Fisher engraved a hilly wooded landscape, filled with wild beasts and birds, in which a profile portrait of himself is out-

Whale. J.F. 1831.

WHALE.

lined by the branches of trees. He also engraved over a hundred and forty wood blocks of animals, reptiles, birds, and insects and arranged them alphabetically, from Adder to Wolf. An appendix added "some short account of the several varieties of the human species." With each cut he gave Biblical references to the creature, information about its species and habits, and often a moral comment in prose or verse. He described the cock, for example, as "A domestic fowl, often called the dung-hill Cock. It is not mentioned in the old Testament, but noticed several times in the new . . ." And he added one of his poems:

> When the Cock crows, remember him,
> Whose look made Peter feel;
> Mourn for your sins, or never dream
> To gain eternal weal.
>
> When the shrill clarion bids you rise,
> Wake up your mental powers,
> For meditation learn to prize
> The cheerful morning hours.

In the introduction to *Scripture Animals* the author wrote: "As respects the Cuts, a few of them are from nature, but most of them are copied, and generally reduced a little . . . I have engraved them myself; and having had no instruction in the art, and but little practice, I can lay claim to no elegance in their appearance. I have endeavored to give a true outline; the filling up must speak for itself." He acknowledged his indebtedness "to Bewick, Mavor, the Cabinet, several Lexicons, and some other works, and to nature." And he added, "In several articles I have given no figures, because I had no patterns within my reach, nor subjects to sketch from."

In most cases he cited his source under the cut as well. The Behemoth (as he called the elephant) is "from Bewick"; the Peacock "I have taken from a little book, I believe anonymous." But "The large black and yellow Spider . . . was drawn from life, August 12, 1826, while on the center of her wheel-net." The figures of the Great Horned Owl and the common Little Owl are "copied from the gleanings of George Edwards," while "the little brown Owl, of the State of Maine," was "drawn from nature, Feb 3, 1832." The earliest dated cut in the book is *Cow. J.F. 1823,* presumably portrayed from life and reminiscent of the cows Fisher liked to show in his painted views.

Fisher had become acquainted with the work of the great English engraver Thomas Bewick (1753-1828) while he was at Harvard, and many of the Scripture animals were copied from cuts in Bewick's

General History of Quadrupeds. A copy was acquired by the Harvard library in 1793, the year when Fisher did his first wood engraving; later he obtained a copy of his own. Besides Bewick and Edwards, Bruce's *Travels* again provided models, as it had for some of the water-color sketches. A dozen or more cuts were based on *A General Collection of Voyages and Travels,* by William Fordyce Mavor, published in London, 1796-1802. From these and other books Fisher helped himself generously to portions of text as well as illustrations. His copying of the latter was not always strictly literal, and his final version was sometimes several steps removed from his first. He writes of transcribing certain pictures—that is, copying his own work; and in preparing his engravings he may have made a copy on the wood block of his copy on paper.

Fisher was indebted to Thomas Bewick not only for "patterns" for many of his cuts but probably also for his very method of making them. It was Bewick who in the late 1700's popularized the method of engraving on the end grain of boxwood with burin or graver instead of cutting along the grain of a softer wood with a knife. His technique, known as white-line engraving, was first used successfully in this country by the New York engraver Dr. Alexander Anderson, who had begun experimenting with it as early as June 1793, when he was a young medical student. Only a month later the young Harvard divinity student Jonathan Fisher was independently experimenting in the same way. While Fisher never acquired Anderson's professional skill, he too was a pioneer in the development of this exacting art.

"Fisher's style of engraving, in the manner of the typical *primitive,* shows the lack of training," Karl Kup has written. "His modeling is poor, that we must admit; his highlights are round circles in the midst of converging engraved lines, as if there was a hole in the print; his proportions of drawing are not always right. But in the handling of the tool, in the application of the whole line, . . . Fisher shows real feeling for the wood block, and real craftsmanship in the execution of his engraving."

While Fisher readily acknowledged his debt to books of engravings, he neglected to give credit to what was apparently his primary source of inspiration for *Scripture Animals.* That, as Miss Byrne discovered, was a book named *Natural History of the Bible; or a description of all the beasts, birds, fishes, insects, reptiles, trees, plants, metals, precious stones etc. mentioned in the Sacred Scriptures. Collected from the best authorities, and alphabetically*

arranged. It was published in Boston in 1793 and the author was Thaddeus Mason Harris (1768-1842), who was librarian of Harvard College from 1791 to 1793. He and Fisher must have known each other, for those were years when Fisher was using the library constantly and was even employed there, and when he was first thinking of doing a book on natural history himself. *Scripture Animals* is very similar to Harris' book in every way, and indeed Fisher had originally intended to use the same title. Unless both men patterned their work on still another source not yet identified, Fisher was heavily indebted to Harris.

To the late twentieth century, familiar with copyright laws and complex restrictions on the use of every kind of recorded material, Jonathan Fisher's outright copying of both words and pictures may seem highly irresponsible. But copying was common practice in his day. The respected Dr. Anderson copied a great deal from Bewick, and Bewick copied a great deal from Buffon. George Edwards, whom Fisher especially favored, was copied not only in prints but in the decoration of textiles and ceramics. Frequently a painting was reproduced in a print and the print in turn was copied in another painting. If copying was accepted among professional artists, it was equally relied upon by amateurs, to whom it was often the only available means of instruction.

As a college student Fisher had begun filling his notebooks with copies of printed texts and illustrations. He frequently transcribed in his shorthand "brief thoughts and meditations" from the classics, and just as he made sketches from book illustrations, so he wrote verses that seem to echo the early romantic poetry of James Thomson or Edward Young, whose books he borrowed from the Harvard library. He went on copying freely and frankly all his life, and while he credited his source more often than not, he also in most cases put his own signature on both engravings and paintings.

To a degree Fisher was typical of the many American amateurs who produced pictures in great quantity and diverse mediums during the late eighteenth century and through most of the nineteenth. He was self-taught, he prepared his own materials and made his own tools, and his very lack of training and sophistication helped to give his work individuality. For him, as for many of his contemporaries, making pictures was more a craft than an art, and he was perhaps more richly endowed with manual dexterity than with artistic sensibility. His natural literal-mindedness made him appreciate simple realism, and that is what he achieved. In his engravings he was usually more successful when he copied the work of others than when he relied on his own invention; in his paintings the opposite is true. His original work with both burin and brush shows a strong feeling for pattern and line, a sense of immediacy, great honesty, and sometimes genuine force. All his work has a personal quality that can only be called charm, and that appeals irresistibly even to his critics.

If other nonacademic artists of Fisher's time made pictures that were more striking in design and color, more dramatic in content, or more accomplished in technique, few if any can have had his wide-ranging interests and his willingness to try his hand at anything. No other comes to mind who produced so many pictures in so many different mediums and with such a diversity of subject matter. In a day when the Yankee was expected to be a Jack-of-all-trades, Fisher outdid most men in versatility.

Still, he was provincial, in outlook as in situation. In the developing industrial age he remained, temperamentally and by training, a man of the eighteenth century. He always had to make contrivance do the work of money, as one of his daughters said; he continued to make things with his hands instead of devising ways to produce them by machine or buying labor-saving novelties, and he continued to think in corresponding terms. The college education he acquired in his twenties developed his tastes and expanded his horizon; it also established standards that he clung to all his life.

Though his views on such matters as education and human rights were advanced, he was essentially conservative. Orthodox in religion, traditional in his approach to science, he was dedicated to both and did not recognize basic disagreements between their adherents which were already growing into open conflict. His taste in literature was for the ancient classics and for Milton and Thomson rather than for Wordsworth or Irving or Cooper. In art, while Cole and his followers of the Hudson River school were painting the grandeurs of nature, Fisher was depicting nature in the particular.

He lived close to nature and he loved it, but not at all in the spirit of the new romanticism. The philosophy of Rousseau did not affect him, if indeed he was acquainted with it. Pascal's conception of man as a thinking reed suited him far better than sentimental ideas about the noble savage and a return to nature: he knew Indians and wilderness at first hand. He was fascinated by all living things, and he expressed his lifelong passion in his own direct, literal way. He consulted some of the great scientific works of the eighteenth century and he learned what he could of the origins and systems of species. If he did not fully understand the controversial theories about the history of the natural world that occupied the enlightened minds of the time, he nevertheless reflected their influence in his personal observations and pictorial records.

The art of Jonathan Fisher is the individual expression of an unusual man. While he was far from being a Bartram or a Franklin, he was a man of his time and theirs. He was inventive and full of intellectual curiosity, and within his own small sphere he exercised his abundant faculties to know and understand the world about him. A vivid personality, lively-minded, many-sided, he was the universal man of a little Maine town, more than a versatile Yankee: in a remote little Maine town he was the universal man.

I Birds and Beasts

Drawn'd and pronted bi Jonrodan Figur, Blehlil Dezember 30. 1800. Prowins uv Maen.

Hast ɟs gívn ɟı **HRRS** strenɟ? Job 39:19.

THE FOX.

THE OTTER.

Plate 3
Although the animals shown might well have been
familiar to Fisher, the plate was undoubtedly
copied from a European source, since the polecat
and squirrel are both European varieties.

THE POLE CAT.

THE SQUIRREL.

THE GUINEA PIG.

Plate 4
COLOR: Several of the plates in Fisher's large notebook, *Natural History,* were devoted to exotic animals copied from Edwards' *Gleanings* in 1795, among them these renderings of a male and female zebra. BLACK AND WHITE: Hart or Stag from *Scripture Animals.*

Zebra femina, sive Asina sylvestris Africana. Drawn from the living animal, belonging to his royal highness the prince of Wales. G. Edwards del. 1751.

ƀı Fɛmʋl Zɛbrʋ.　Zebre Femelle.

Happied ʇı proʋʋ ʋʋʋ befʋr June 19. 1795.

Zebra mas, sive Asina sylvestris Africanus, drawn from a staff'd skin in the royal College of Physicians, London. George Edwards delin. June 1751.

ƀı Mʋl Zɛbrʋ.　The Male Zebra.
Jıs anımal　Zebra Male.

Plate 5
COLOR: Bear and Catamount, two separate plates
from *Natural History,* the former signed and dated
February 16, 1795, and inscribed "Drawn to a scale
of 1½ inches to a foot." The latter, to a scale
of 1¼ inches to a foot, was drawn from life June
17, 1793, and "transferred" February 17, 1795.
BLACK AND WHITE: Wolf, also from *Natural History.*

ᏓᎢ Wolf. ׃זְאֵב לύχος. *Loup.* Wolf.

From the Cabinet, or Natural History of Birds, Beasts &c. enlarged & painted

By Jonathan Fisher,

Bluehill Oct. 17. 1810.

Jonathan Fisher delin. et pinx. Jonathan Fisher delin. & pinx. 1795.

Drawn to a scale of 1½ inch to a foot, Februere 16ᵈ. 1795

бı Bęr. דוב sar דֹב. Aρϰτος. Ursus. L'Ours.

The Bear.

Jonathan Fisher delin. et pinx.

Drawn to a scale of 1¼ inch to a foot 17ᵗʰ Juan 1793; transfered Feb. 17ᵈ. 1795.

бı Katʊmɛnt.   Le Chatpard.

The Catamount.

Plate 6

The Lion and the Lioness. The color plate is inscribed, "Drawn from nature, and painted Feb. 20, 1795." Both it and the woodcut from *Scripture Animals* were based on Fisher's view of a lion brought from Africa to New York and thence to Boston, where it was exhibited in 1794. The Lioness, which looks like a small dog, was copied from Hill's *Natural History* in February 1795 at "Cambridge, N.E."

Drʒn fram natur, and printed Feb. 20. 1795. By Jonatan Fiʃur. Ɖ livʒ animal, ƕicɖ ɖis draft iz deʒined to reprezent, waz mʒl, ƕen a ƕelp, in ɖ wodz av Gorz, in Afreka, and brʒt ɖis to Nu york; in ɖ fʒl av 1794, & wintur folowʒ he woz exibited in Boston; ƕen biiŋ betwiʒn 4 & 5 yerz old, he woz upwurdz av 3 fit hi, & abʌt 7 fit fram nostrilz to teal.

Ƃi Liun. אַרְיֵה. Λέων. Leo. Le Lion.

Ɖ smʒl ƕʌ av ɖ liunes, reprezented az in ɖ Ɉnos; kopied fram Hilz Nat. Hist. and printed bi Jonotan Fiʃur, Feb. 23. 1795, at Ɍrombrij, N. J.

Ƃi Liunes. לְבִיָא. Λέαινα. Leæna. La Lionne.

Plate 7
Elephant and Rhinoceros. These behemoths must
have fascinated Fisher, who copied two versions,
this derived from Edwards, and another probably
based on Bewick, into his *Natural History* notebook.
Still a third version of the Rhinoceros
appears in his small untitled notebook, under
the heading "Natural History."

drawn from a young Elephant in London; the teeth are added to complete the figure.

61 Elıfant.   Elephant.

Published Sept. 14. 1752. Geor. Edwards Del. & Sculp.
The Female Rhinoceros, drawn from the life in London, 1752.

61 Rinasıras.   Le Rhinoceros.

Plate 8

COLOR: The Mongoose and the Gerbil, both again
copied from Edwards in Fisher's large notebook.
In later years he copied the Mongoose in oil,
and he engraved for *Scripture Animals* a small
cut of the Jerboa, as he then captioned it, "from
George Edwards." BLACK AND WHITE: Hyaena,
from Fisher's untitled notebook.

Natural History.

Beaſts.

Jonathan Fisher
1793.

THE HYÆNA OF AFRICA.

Taken from Bruce's Travels; drawn to a ſcale of ¼ an inch to a foot.
Length from noſe to rump 5 feet 9 inches; height from the
ſole of the forefoot to the top of the shoulder 3 feet 9 inches.
Color; Back & tail reddish brown; body in general yellow-
ish brown.

Sept. 23. 1793.

Ƃı Mʌɾgꝺz.   Le Mongous.

Ƃı Jurbɔꝟ.   Le Gerbua.

This animal, which is one of the first of the genus of Monkies, is supposed to come the nearest in its outward shape to man. The old ones are said, by many of our voyagers to Africa and India, to be near six feet high, when standing, or walking erect.

The subject from which this figure was drawn, is now preserved in the British Museum, in London; it was a young one, and about two feet and an half high when it died: it was first soaked in spirits of wine, then dried, and set up in the action I have given it, the draught being taken before its parts were too much dried or fallen in. It differed from the generality in having no tail, or callous skin behind, to sit on, as most Monkies have; and in having the head rounder, and more human-like, than most of its kind: the forehead was high and rising, the nose flat, the teeth much resembled those of men; the hair from the neck inclined upwards round to the fore-head and the sides of the face, which was without hair; the ears were also naked, and much of the human make. (See the profile head, which gives the manner of the growth of the hair.) It had two nipples, situated as in man: the face and naked parts of the paws were of a swarthy flesh-colour: the body and limbs were covered with a loose, shaggy, reddish-brown hair, thicker on the hinder parts, and thinner before: the hair from the hand to the elbow inclined towards the elbow.

About fifty years ago was published an anatomical description, by Edward Tyson, M.D. of this same animal, which he calls the Pigmy, wherein he has given figures of it: and since him, A.D. 1738, a figure was published of one that was brought from the coast of Africa, called Chimp-anzee, and shewn in London; which print is inscribed to Sir Hans Sloane. But neither of these prints were satisfactory to me, who had seen the above-described, which was a female, with one other (a male) now in my hands; both agreeing exactly in every part, but what distinguishes the sexes: for which reason I have published this figure, the original whereof was with great care done by me, to be preserved amongst the drawings of animals, in the Museum of the late Sir Hans Sloane, Bart. now in the British Museum. I believe them all to be natives of Africa; though there are voyagers to India that describe something like them. In a book of prints by P. Vander Aa, bookseller at Leiden, (which prints I believe are gathered from voyagers) he gives two plates, 11 and 77, of what he calls Satyrs, or Orang Outang. Capt. Beeckman, in his Voyage to Borneo, Lond. 1718, has figured and described one near of kin to this, but not the same: he was borrowed the former name, but has otherwise wrote it Oran Ootan, which, he says, in their language signifies Man of the Woods. He says, they have no hair but on those parts where it grows on human bodies: if this be true, it is nearer the human species than what is here figured.

'Ƀı Man ᴧᴠ ƒı Wodz.   L'Homme Sauvage.

Ƀıs animal, ŵiđn iz wun ᴧᴠ ƒı furst
ᴧᴠ ƒı jenus ᴧᴠ Munkiz, iz sup
ozed tu kum nrest in its stwund
froʃ tu man. Ƀi old wunz ᴧᴘsed,
bi mene ᴧᴠ ᴅr vᴧᴧ̈jurz tu Af-
rḁkn, tu bı nɛr six fet hᴘ, ŵen
standıŋ ᴧᴘ ŵᴧkıŋ erɛkt. – Ƀı
subjekt from ŵiđn ƀis figur
wᴧᴠ Druᴘn, iz nᴧ prezurved in
ƀı Brítiʃ muzeum, in Lun-
dun. It wᴧᴢ ᴧ yuŋ wun, &
ᴧbᴘt ƀrʒ fet ᴧnd ᴧn hɛf hᴘ,
ŵen it died. –– It frᴘp ᴧ-
zembled most ᴧfurᴢ ᴧᴠ ƀı

On suppose que cet animal, qui
est un des premiers du genre
singe, est celui de tous, qui ap-
proche le plus de l'homme par
l'extérieur. Plusieurs Anglois,
qui ont voyagé en Afrique &
aux Indes, rapportent que ceux
qui ont fait leur vrüe, ont près
de six pieds de haut, quand ils
se tiennent de bout, & qu'ils
marchent sur leur. ᵖⁱᵉᵈˢ de Derière.
Le sujet d'après lequel cette
figure a été deſsinée, est à pré-
sent dans cette ville de Londres,

61 St. Jago Muykı.   Le Singe *de l'Iſle de* St. Jaques.

The black Maucauco from Madagascar.　　　George Edwards delin & sculp.
A.D. 1756.

61 Blak Mʌkʌko. 1795.　　　Le Maucauco Noir.

george Edwards delin 1752.   The male Cagui Minor of Piso, natural size

Not, ye first ez tre r drwn napur th shw.

Ft Sanglin or Cagui Minor,   Le Sanglin ou Cagui Minor.

Iz n spefi'z w animal w't   Cette sorte d'animal est une espèce de

Plate 13
The Little Ant-Eater. Again Fisher repeated
Edwards' inscription on the plate, noting that
the animal was "Drawn near of the natural
size." The text below goes on to indicate
that the sloth-toed creature was about
the size of a squirrel.

An animal
from the Spanish main in America
Drawn near of the natural size

Geo. Edwards Delin & Sc. 1754.

61 Litl Ant-Etur.   Le Mangeur de Fourmis Minor.

Natural History.

Flies.

Jonathan Fisher
1793

3. Two views of the common
house, or window fly, drawn
to the full size July 1. 1793

1. A view of the large
brown horse fly; drawn to the full size,
June 27th. 1793. — 2. The head magnified.

4. A view of the great
black horse fly; drawn
to the full size from
the life at Roxbury;
August 13th. 1793.

5. American Locust; from nature,
at Bluehill, Nov. 13. 1821. Its organ
of music consists of two bladders
in the breast, and a crevice
between the breast and abdomen,
thro' which the wind is emitted.

Natural History.

Butterflies.

Jonathan Fisher 1793

1. Two views of a species of butterfly, drawn from the life,
June 26th. 1793; taken to the full bigness.

2. A view of the common
yellow butterfly, drawn to
the full size, July 1. 1793.

3. Brown butterfly, from
nature, Bluehill Nov. 13. 1821.

By Jon. Fisher.

Natural History.

Bugs.

Jonathan Fisher 1793

1.2. Two views of the yellow, purple bellied bug,
3. One wing expanded. Drawn June 27th. 1793.
taken to the full size; from the life.

4. A view of the small
red, black spotted bug,
drawn to the full size
June 27th. 1793.

6. The little orange colored,
double spotted bug; drawn
to the full size Sep. 24. 1793.

5. A view of the large, chestnut
colored, horned dors bug; drawn
to the full size; June 27th. 1793.

Je strinted Limpet.

Je stiri Limpet.

Je beked Limpet.

Je szrikuulated pupur Naztilus.

Je lizn Br Sel.

Je grnt Br Sel.

Stompsus sp.2.
Dentrlyum sp.1.

Je pupur Naztilus.

Je Dng taD Sel.

Je strinted IsD Sel.

Je litl Dik Naztilus.

Je Belted Snrl.

Je wid mxf'd smrl.

Je prikhli Snrl.

Je goldn mxf'd Snrl.

Je Ekuminted Haklus.

Je tsded Nerit Snrl.

Je Hzrnuu Amonis Snrl.

Je Muf Trokus.

Je prickhli Trokus.

Je mitur Sel.

Je Isr rv Brbel Sel.

Je ruf mxf'd Baxinum.

Je Nedl Sel.

Je lizn mxfed Turbo.

Je vis Admiral. Je Admiral.
Je Tigur Sel.

Je ruf Skrue Sel.

Kopied from Hilz Natural Histori. April 1795.
hi Jemsdan Tifur.

Brasilian Macaw.

Copied from George Edwards, and painted by Jonathan Fisher, Bluehill, Maine, March 16, 1841.

COLOR: Baltimore Oriole and Bird of Paradise
from *Varietas*. BLACK AND WHITE: an exotic and
a perhaps more familiar bird from *Scripture
Animals*. The oriole Fisher might have seen in
New England, although the rather formal composition makes it seem likely that he copied it
from an unknown source. The two views of the
Bird of Paradise were "taken from the Royal
Society." In his diary he noted that they were
painted December 18, 1792.

CORMORANT.

Baltimore Oriole.

Plate 18
COLOR: Black and White Butcher Bird, 1815.
BLACK AND WHITE: Heron from *Scripture Animals*.
The "small 'buturfli' from China" was,
according to Edwards, called the Black and
White Butcher-Fly, a pleasant coincidence
of name, although the two winged creatures
were in no other way associated.

George Edwards delin   *Jonathan Fisher Pinx 1815*

ƀı Blak and Wit Bɔʃur Burd,

and ᵥ Smᴂl Buturﬄi fram Ꮹinᵥ. Ɉ Fiʃur pınx.

The ash coloured hawk & the little brown lizard, from Geo. Edwards

Ash colored Hawk, Brown Lizard.

Copied from George Edwards, and painted by
Jonathan Fisher, Bluehill, 1840.

Plate 20
The Great Horned Owl from Athens, 1840.
This bird, as Fisher carefully copied in script
beneath the stump, is "supposed to be the bird
sacred to the goddess Minerva." He copied it
on the block just as he had in water color, so
that the woodcut in *Scripture Animals* is
printed in reverse.

The Great Horned Owl *from* Athens.

Jon. Fisher pinx. from Geo. Edwards. 1840.

The Little Owl.

Copied from the gleanings of Geo. Edwards by Jon. Fisher,

Painted, March, 1841.

The crow'ed eagle from the coast of guinea

The Crown'd Eagle.

From the coast of Guinea. J.F. 1840.

II Flora

Plate 23
COLOR: Navigation or The Mariner's Compass, 1791.
BLACK AND WHITE: Cardinal Points and Calculation
of Chimney Height. All from Fisher's notebook
titled *Mathematics.*

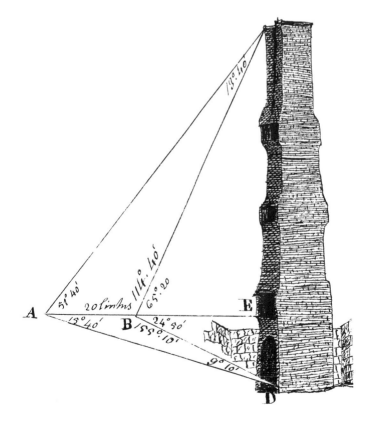

NAVIGATION.

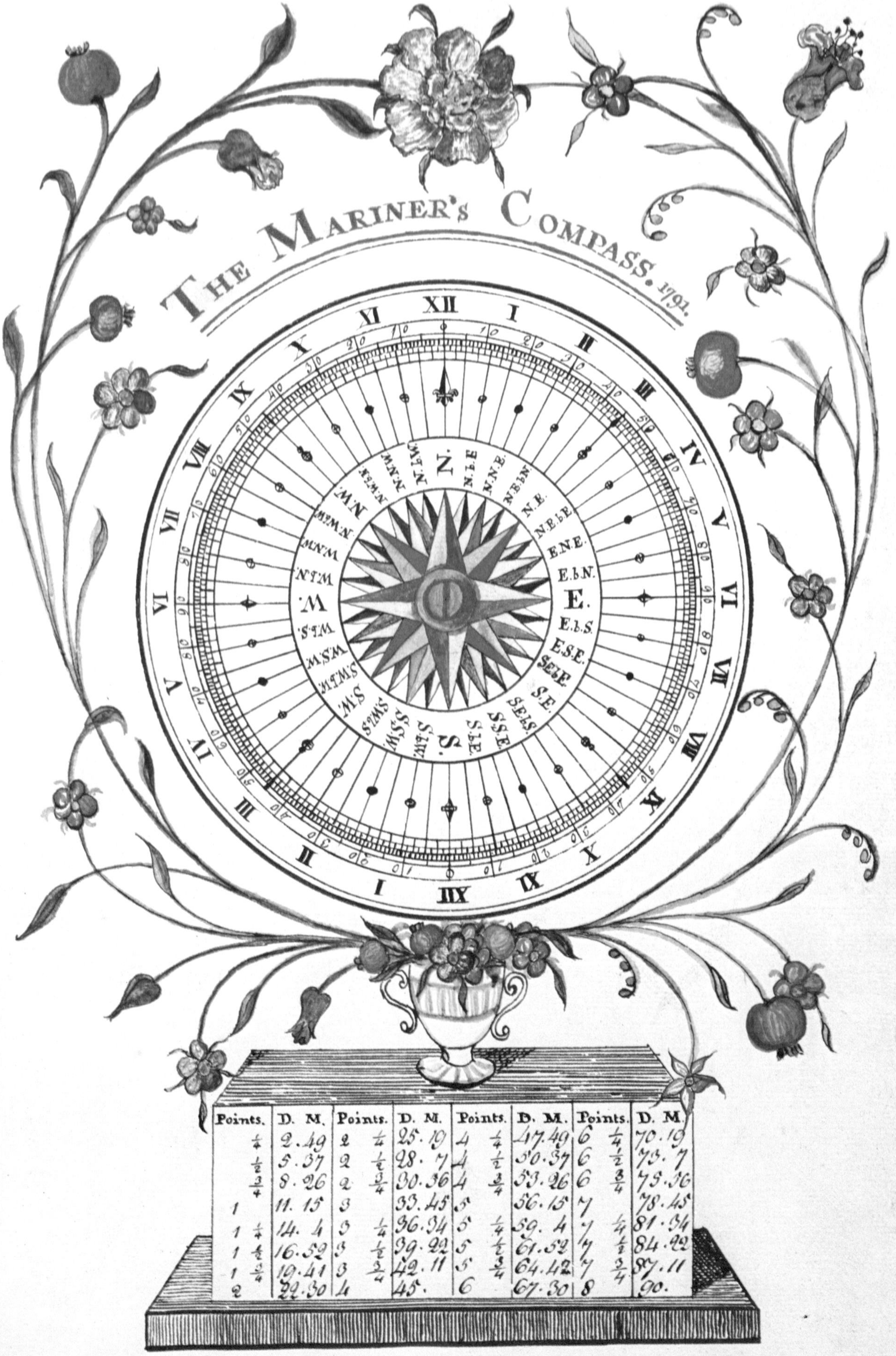

THE MARINER'S COMPASS. 1792.

Points.	D. M.	Points.	D. M.	Points.	D. M.	Points.	D. M.
¼	2.49	2 ¼	25.19	4 ¼	47.49	6 ¼	70.19
½	5.37	2 ½	28. 7	4 ½	50.37	6 ½	73. 7
¾	8.26	2 ¾	30.36	4 ¾	53.26	6 ¾	75.56
1	11.15	3	33.45	5	56.15	7	78.45
1 ¼	14. 4	3 ¼	36.34	5 ¼	59. 4	7 ¼	81.34
1 ½	16.52	3 ½	39.22	5 ½	61.52	7 ½	84.22
1 ¾	19.41	3 ¾	42.11	5 ¾	64.42	7 ¾	87.11
2	22.30	4	45.	6	67.30	8	90.

Plate 24

COLOR: The Plain Scale, 1791. BLACK AND WHITE:
Heights and Distances. Fisher adorned *Mathematics*
with colorful sprigs, seemingly painted for pure
pleasure, and also with illustrations of mathematical
problems, based on familiar sites on the Harvard
campus of his time.

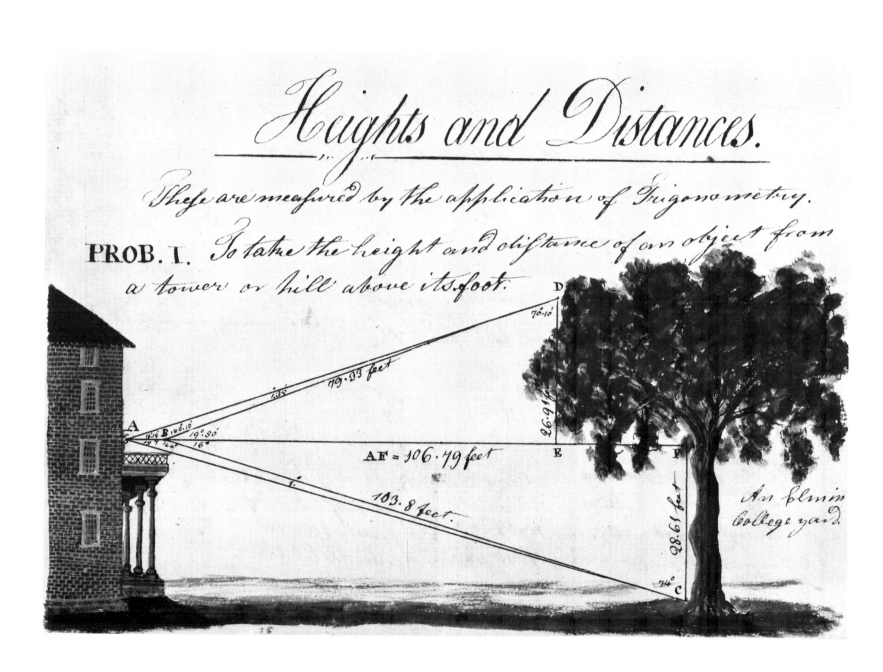

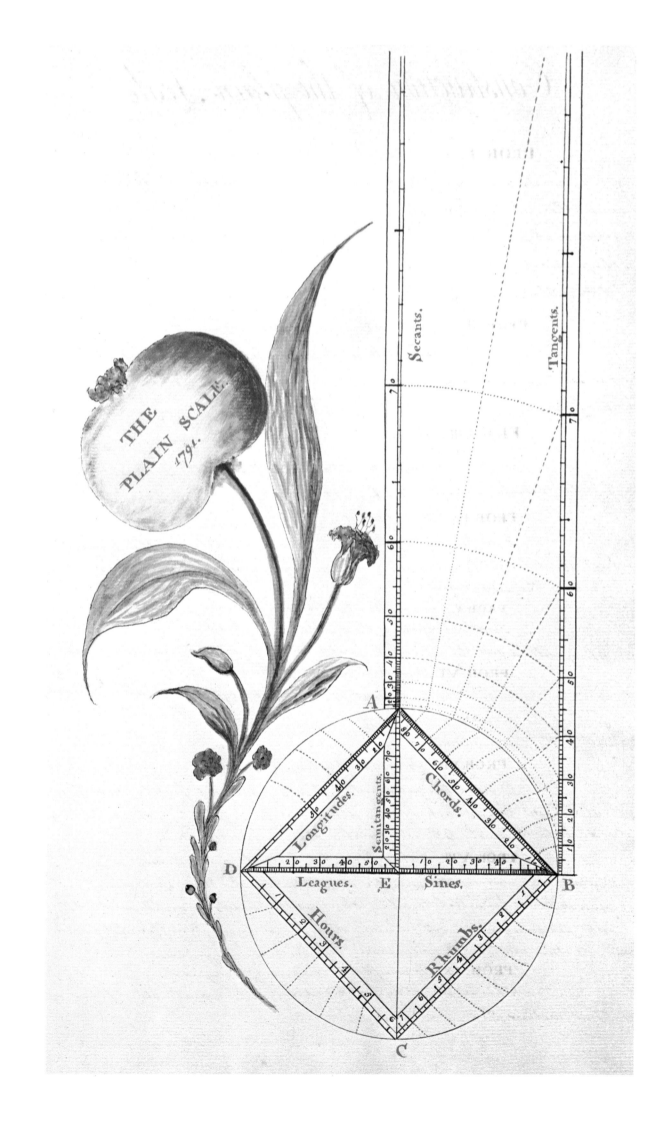

THE
PLAIN SCALE.
1791.

Secants.

Tangents.

Chords.

Longitudes.

Semitangents.

A

Leagues.   E   Sines.   B

D

Hours.

Rhumbs.

C

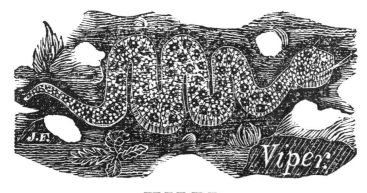

VIPER.

61 Apl-Survis. Sorbum. The Apple-Service. La Corme.

Plate 26

COLOR: Peach BLACK AND WHITE:
Nuts, 1821. Both from the untitled notebook.
Although many of his paintings of birds and
beasts were copied from printed sources, Fisher's
botanical studies were mostly "drawn from life,"
the flowers and fruits with which he was familiar
in his own garden and farm.

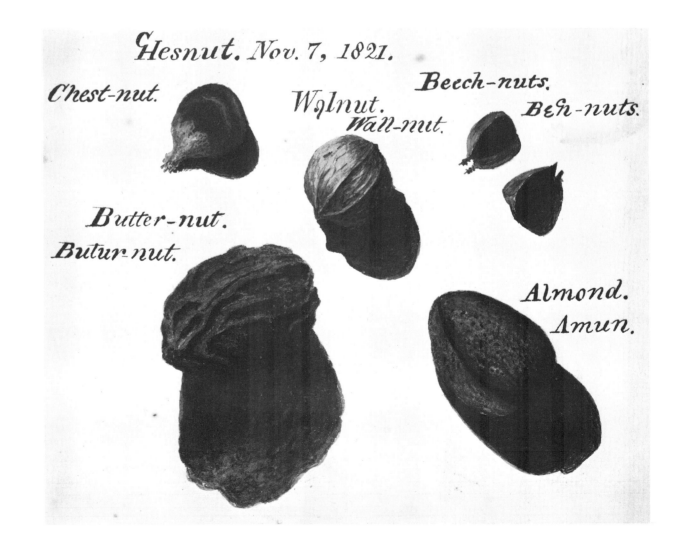

ნ Rariნ, an urli Peň.

Drżn & printed bi Jamodan Fiſher, Nov. 5. 1798.

Plate 27

The Hand of a Boy with a Distempered Skin, and A Branch of the Common-Service Tree. A rather grisly picture in Fisher's *Natural History* was copied in 1795 from Edwards' *Gleanings*, with transcription of Edwards' text, which in turn was taken from a long account of a curious medical case printed in *Philosophical Transactions*, No. 424, of the Royal Society of London.

A small pes ov ti skin ov ti hand, her drawn, magnified.

Main d'un petit Garçon, qui avoit une Maladie de la peau. Branche de
Cormier commun.   Sorbus Torminalis.

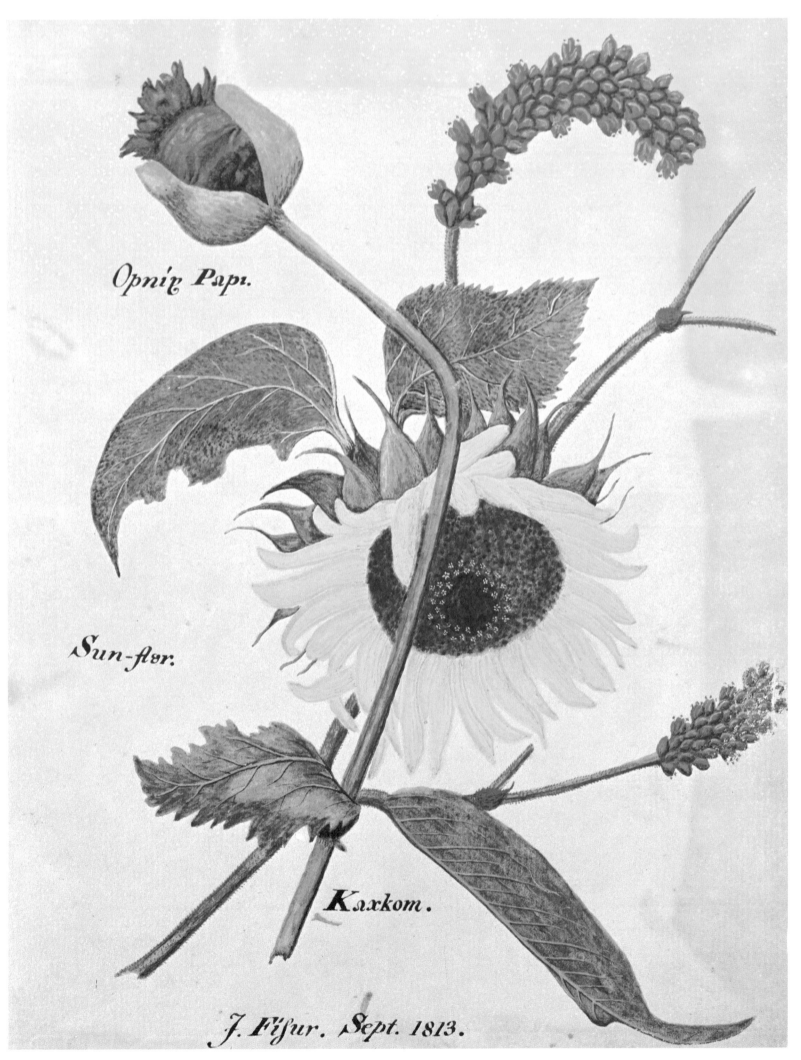

Opníʏ Papι.

Sun-flɵr.

Kɪxkom.

J. Fiſur. Sept. 1813.

Plate 29

COLOR: Garden Pea, 1810, and Strawberry Plant.
BLACK AND WHITE: Frog. Fisher noted that this
was a "Figure from Life." The common frog, he
wrote in *Scripture Animals,* "…feeds on common
flies, butterflies, &c. which come to the water's
edge to drink. They move towards the little insect
with the utmost caution, till within due distance,
then give a sudden leap, and seize it in an
instant. I have frequently amused myself in
seeing them in this manner take their prey."

Garden Pe. Garden Pea. *J. Fisher pinx. Sep. 29. 18*

J. Fisher pinx. 1810. Sept. 29.

Plate 30
Larkspur, "Drawn from nature, and painted by
Jonathan Fisher. Bluhill October, 1810."
Fisher's enjoyment of brilliant, intense colors
is equally evident in his paintings of exotic
birds and in the flowers he chose to record
in water color.

Larkspur. Drzn frnm nntur,

and painted by Jonathan Fisher.

Blthil Aktobur, 1810

London Pride. J. Fisher, 1820.

Plate 32

COLOR: Carrot, 1808, from the untitled notebook.
BLACK AND WHITE: Canker Worm and Caterpillar
from *Scripture Animals.* If Fisher saw the hand of
God in the wondrous shape of a carrot, he was
equally aware of the importance of the worm in
the garden:

> The creeping vermin, feeble in our eyes,
> And reptiles base, which men in scorn
>   despise,
> Are oft commission'd by a jealous God
> To be for judgment, his tremendous rod.

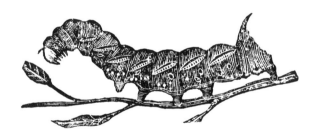

CANKER WORM.

Carrot.

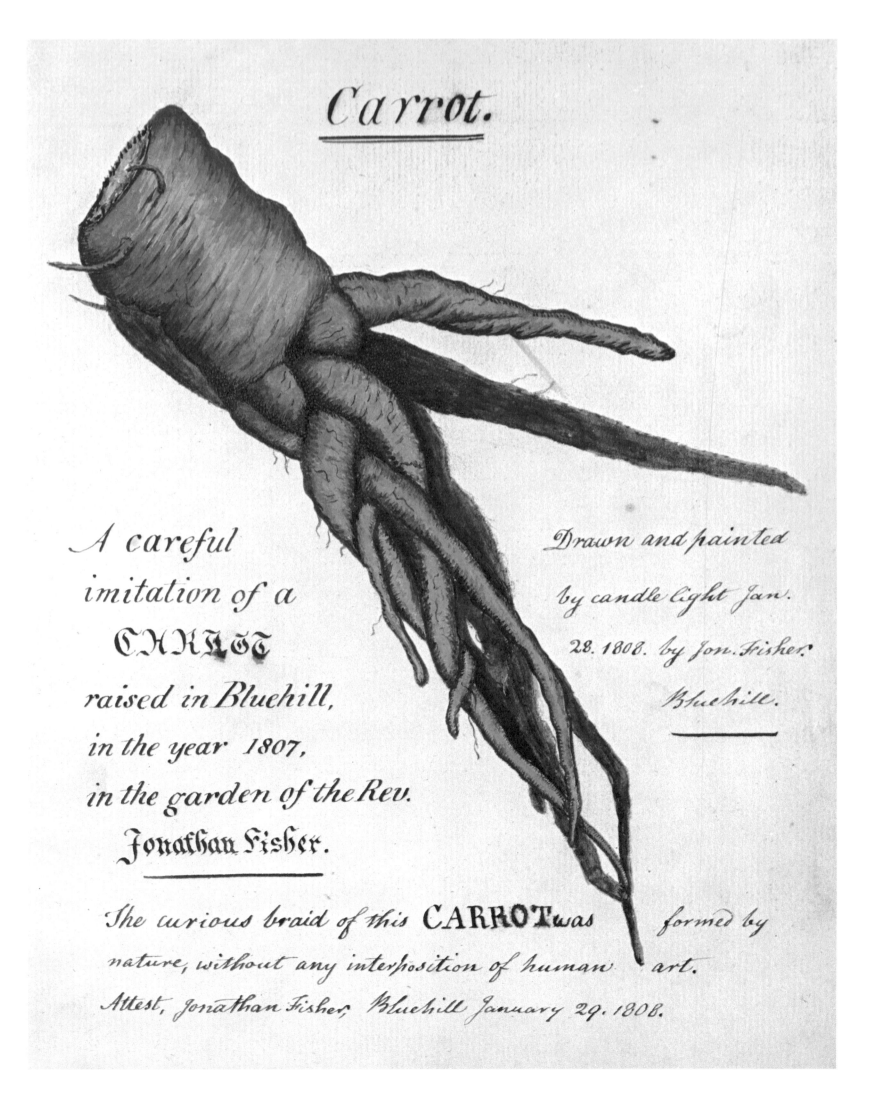

A careful imitation of a 𝕮𝕳𝕽𝕽𝕺𝕿 raised in Bluehill, in the year 1807, in the garden of the Rev. Jonathan Fisher.

Drawn and painted by candle light Jan. 28. 1808. by Jon. Fisher. Bluehill.

The curious braid of this CARROT was formed by nature, without any interposition of human art. Attest, Jonathan Fisher, Bluehill January 29. 1808.

Plate 33
This floral spray terminating in a somewhat
remarkable blue carnation or pink fills most
of the page headed "Elements of Geometry"
in Fisher's *Mathematics* notebook.

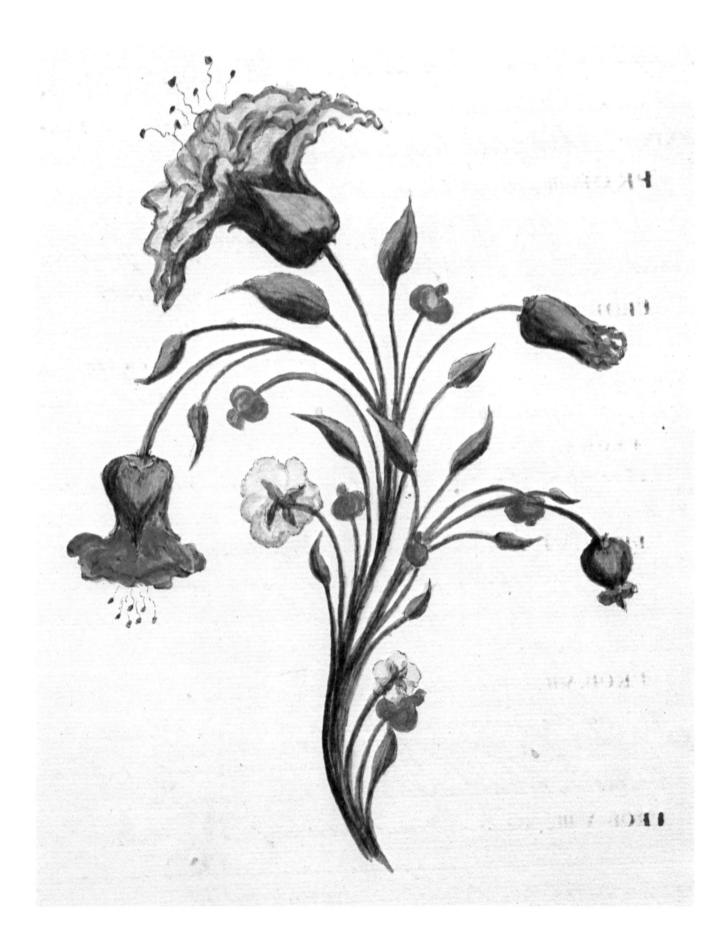

III Paintings in Oil

SPRING

Youth is the Spring, when those celestial flowers
Shoot bud and Blossom in the cultur'd mind,
Which give to life a Summer free from blight,
And yield an Autumn rich in holy fruit,
Matur'd, and waiting joyful harvest home.

J. Fisher Pinxit, Bluehill, May, 1822, from Lemire.

Plate 35
Four birds. Oil on canvas, 19½ by 26½ inches.
Signed and dated October 1820. *Jonathan Fisher
Memorial, Inc.*

King-Wood-Pecker,
Golden-Crown'd W-Pecker,
Slate-Colored Snow-Bird,
Seeder. Drawn from nature.
Oct. 1820. J. Fisher.
Maine.

Plate 38

A North West Prospect of Nassau Hall with a
Front View of the President's House in New
Jersey. Oil on canvas, 26½ by 59½ inches.
Signed and dated 1807. After an engraving
of 1764 by Henry Dawkins. *Princeton University.*

Front View of the President's House in New Jersey. J. Fisher pinx.t Thomas Clark sculpt Feb.y 1764.

List of Works

The following list of Fisher's paintings in oil and in water color records all the surviving examples that it has been possible to locate. Others may well exist. Some that are referred to in Fisher's writings have not been found—a view of the Lowell house in Cambridge and one of the Episcopal Church, to name two. Citations of "Bail's check list" refer to the list of Fisher's Harvard views in *Views of Harvard; a pictorial record to 1860*, by Hamilton Vaughan Bail, Cambridge, Harvard University Press, 1949.

The list of publications is derived from the Sinclair Hamilton Collection of early American illustrated books in the Princeton University Library; it names all the books presently known to include wood engravings by Fisher. His published works also include at least one wood engraving of 1796 printed in the Dedham, Massachusetts, newspaper *The Minerva*; and two illustrations of the hanging of criminals engraved for broadsides which were printed in Maine, one in 1811 by A. H. Holland of Buckstown, the other in 1824 by E. Brewster of Bangor.

In addition to the items listed below there are numerous unframed and uncatalogued drawings and unpublished wood engravings in the collections of the Jonathan Fisher Memorial, Inc., at Blue Hill, Maine, and of the William A. Farnsworth Library and Art Museum at Rockland, Maine.

For invaluable assistance in the preparation of the following lists I am indebted to Constance M. Greiff of The Pyne Press.

Paintings in oil

1. HARVARD COLLEGE BUILDINGS   Plate 38
   Oil on canvas, 19.4 by 26 inches.
   Inscribed, not in Fisher's hand: "Parson Fisher 1790";
   almost certainly painted later. Bail's check list a.
   Harvard Club of New York City.

2. HARVARD COLLEGE
   Oil on canvas, 19⅞ by 27 inches.
   Jonathan Fisher Memorial, Inc., Blue Hill, Maine.

3. HARVARD, HOLLIS, AND MASSACHUSETTS HALLS
   Oil on canvas, 19⅝ by 26⅝ inches.
   Bail's check list i; then owned by Roland M. Howard.
   William A. Farnsworth Library and Art Museum, Rockland, Maine.

4. NASSAU HALL AND THE PRESIDENT'S HOUSE   Plate 39
   Oil on canvas, 26½ by 59½ inches.
   Inscribed: "A North West Prospect of Nassau Hall
   with a Front View of the President's house in New Jersey.
   J. Fisher Pinxit from an Old Print, Feb. 1807."
   Princeton University, Princeton, New Jersey.

5. FOUR BIRDS   Plate 35
   Oil on canvas, 19½ by 26½ inches.
   Inscribed: "King Wood Pecker/Golden Crown'd W-pecker
   Slate-color'd Snow-bird/Seeder/Drawn from nature Oct. 1820
   J. Fisher, Maine."
   Jonathan Fisher Memorial.

6. MONGOOSE
   Oil on panel, 12 by 9⅝ inches.
   Farnsworth Museum.

7. RED COW   Plate 36
   Oil on canvas, 23⅛ by 20¼ inches.
   Farnsworth Museum.

8. VIEW OF DEDHAM, MASSACHUSETTS   Plate 40
   Oil on canvas, 19¾ by 26½ inches.
   Traditionally dated c. 1790; probably painted 1798.
   Farnsworth Museum.

9. HOUSE AND LANDSCAPE
   Oil on panel, 13⅜ by 18¼ inches.
   Probably the view of the Avery House, Dedham,
   which Fisher painted in 1803.
   Farnsworth Museum.

10. PLINY BINGHAM'S, DEDHAM
    Oil on canvas, 19 by 26 inches.
    Inscribed: "J. Fisher 1822."
    Mrs. Theodore Babbitt.

11. SPRING
    Oil on canvas, 26½ by 20 inches.
    Inscribed: "SPRING
    Youth is the Spring, when those celestial flowers
    Shou'd bud and Blossom in the cultur'd mind,
    Which give to life a Summer free from blight,
    And yield an Autumn rich in holy fruit,
    Matur'd, and waiting joyful harvest home.
    J. Fisher Pinxit, Bluehill, May 1822, from Lemire."
    Jonathan Fisher Memorial.

12. SELF-PORTRAIT   Plate 34
    Oil on canvas, 32¼ by 27¾ inches.
    Inscribed, lower left: "Rev. Jonathan Fisher Bluehill Maine";
    lower right: "Jonᵃ. Fisher pinx. Aetatis 56 1824."
    Jonathan Fisher Memorial.

13. SELF-PORTRAIT

Page 15

Oil on canvas, 33¼ by 28½ inches.
Inscribed, lower left: "Rev. Jonathan Fisher Bluehill Maine";
lower right: "Jon. Fisher Pinx. Aetatis 56 1824."
Bangor Theological Seminary, Bangor, Maine.

14. SELF-PORTRAIT

Oil on canvas, 31½ by 27½ inches.
Inscribed, lower left: "Rev. Jonathan Fisher Bluehill Maine.";
lower right: "Jonathan Fisher pinx. 1824 Aetatis 56
Transcr. 1838."
Blue Hill Congregational Church, Blue Hill, Maine.

15. SELF-PORTRAIT

Oil on canvas, 31 by 27 inches.
Inscribed, lower left: "Rev. Jonathan Fisher Bluehill Maine";
lower right: "Jon. Fisher pinx. 1824 Aetatis 56
Transcr. 1838."
Robert L. Fisher.

16. A MORNING VIEW OF BLUEHILL VILLAGE

Jacket illus.

Oil on canvas, 25½ by 52 inches.
Inscribed, lower right: "A morning View of Bluehill Village.
Sept. 1824 Jon. Fisher pinx."
Farnsworth Museum.

17. THE LATTER HARVEST

Plate 37

Oil on canvas, 19⅞ by 26½ inches.
Inscribed: "J. Fisher P./The Latter Harvest. 1832
Thou crownest the year with thy goodness. Ps. 65 ii."
Farnsworth Museum.

18. GETHSEMANE

Oil on panel, 22⅞ by 19½ inches.
Inscribed: "From a print engraved by W. Fathorne,
Enlarged & Painted by J. Fisher, 1838."
Farnsworth Museum.

19. DESCENT FROM THE CROSS

Oil on canvas, 21¾ by 27¼ inches.
Farnsworth Museum.

20. SCENE FROM "PAUL AND VIRGINIA"

Oil on canvas, 25¾ by 52 inches.
Inscribed, lower right: "Bluehill, Maine."
Farnsworth Museum.

21. THE SERVICE MAID
    Oil on panel, 20½ by 23 inches.
    Inscribed:
    "Miss Betsy Hussy, with her pail and broom
    From honest labor here comes trudging home
    'Tis better far to earn the bread we eat
    Than to live idly with the rich and great
    J. Fisher pinx., Feb. 1847."
    Farnsworth Museum.

22. JULIA AND COSSET
    Oil on panel, 19¾ by 22¾ inches.
    Inscribed:
    "Drink, drink my little lamb, the stream
    Is free for you and me;
    Tho' cheap the chrystal draught may be
    It yields the richest glee.
    J. Fisher pinx. 1847."
    Farnsworth Museum.

23. VIEW ALONG THE MAINE COAST
    Oil on canvas, 26½ by 46½ inches.
    Attributed by the owner to Jonathan Fisher.
    Hirschl & Adler Galleries, Inc., New York City

Paintings in Water Color

Views of Harvard

1. HOLLIS HALL
   Oval, 8.4 by 10.15 inches, within a black border;
   on a sheet about 20 by 30 inches
   with "orthographical projections" of the building
   (Fisher's Mathematical Thesis).
   Inscribed: "To the Governors of Harvard College
   This Perspective View of Hollis Hall
   Is Humbly Presented by their dutiful Pupil, Jonathan Fisher.
   September 27th. 1791."
   Bail's check list b.
   Harvard University Archives.

2. HOLLIS, HARVARD, AND MASSACHUSETTS HALLS
   Oval, 9½ by 12½ inches, on rectangular sheet.
   Inscribed: "Sketched from nature Sept. 1793 & painted Nov. 1793
   By Jonathan Fisher, at Cambridge, Massachusetts.
   Hollis, Harvard, and Massachusetts Halls." Bail's check list c.
   Boston Athenaeum.

3. HOLLIS, HARVARD, AND MASSACHUSETTS HALLS
   Oval, 9 by 12 inches, on rectangular sheet.
   Inscribed: "Hollis, Harvard, and Massachusetts Halls,
   at Cambridge, N. England.
   Jonathan Fisher del. et pinx. 1794 No. 6."
   The windowpanes of the buildings are pin-pricked. Bail's check list d.
   Harvard University Archives.

4. HOLLIS, HARVARD, AND MASSACHUSETTS HALLS
   9½ by 13 inches.
   Inscribed: "Hollis, Harvard, and Massachusetts Halls
   at Cambridge in N. England.
   Jonathan Fisher del. et pinx. 1794."
   Mrs. Theodore C. Diller.

5. HARVARD HALL
   Oval, 10½ by 13½ inches, on rectangular sheet.
   Inscribed: "Jonathan Fisher pinx. 1795.
   Harvard Hall in the University of Cambridge, New England."
   Bail's check list f. This and Nos. 6 and 7 were evidently
   made as a series.
   Boston Athenaeum.

6. HOLLIS HALL
   Oval, 10½ by 13½ inches, on rectangular sheet.
   Inscribed: "Jonathan Fisher pinx. 1795.
   Hollis Hall in the University of Cambridge, New England."
   Bail's check list e.
   Boston Athenaeum.

7. MASSACHUSETTS HALL
   Oval, 10½ by 13½ inches, on rectangular sheet.
   Inscribed: "Jonathan Fisher pinx. 1795.
   Massachusetts Hall in the University of Cambridge, New England."
   Bail's check list g.
   Boston Athenaeum.

8. HOLLIS HALL
   Bail's check list h: unlocated; size unknown;
   believed to be 1795.

9. HARVARD HALL
    Oval 8.15 by 12.4 inches.
    Inscribed in Fisher's early phonetic shorthand: "Harvurd Hal."
    Probably Bail's check list j, then owned by Benton L. Rude.
    Colby College, Waterville, Maine.

10. MASSACHUSETTS HALL
    Oval, 9¾ by 13 inches, on rectangular sheet.
    Inscribed: "Massachusetts Hall at Harvard."
    Perhaps Bail's check list b, then unlocated.
    Farnsworth Museum.

11. HARVARD COLLEGE
    Details lacking.
    Mrs. Albert F. Steinman.

Notebooks

1. A COLLECTION OF NATURAL HISTORY
    Title lettered in Fisher's early shorthand.
    32 pages, 17 by 11 inches, leatherbound.
    Water-color sketches of animals, birds, fruit, flowers,
    shells; dated 1795, 1810, 1840, 1841; 3 pages blank.
    The first 14 pages, all dated 1795, were copied from Edwards'
    Gleanings of Natural History, including inscriptions on
    plates and two columns of text; 6 other sketches were copied
    from Edwards without text, some dated 1840, 1841.
    Jonathan Fisher Memorial.

    Plates 4, 5, 6, 8, 9,
    10, 11, 12, 13,
    15, 16, 18, 19,
    20, 20, 21, 22, 25,
    27, 29, 30; facing
    Plate 8

2. MATHEMATICS
    Title page dated 1791.
    96 pages, 12¾ by 7¾ inches, leatherbound.
    Pages headed: Elements of Geometry, Plain Trigonometry,
    Heights and Distances, Surveying, Navigation, Plane Sailing,
    Traverse Sailing, Oblique Sailing, Parallel Sailing, Middle
    Latitude Sailing, Mercator's Sailing, Mercator's Chart,
    Dialing. Copiously illustrated with diagrams and decorations,
    many in black and red ink, some in water color,
    dated 1791 and 1793.
    Jonathan Fisher Memorial.

    Plates 23, 24, 33;
    facing Plates 23, 24;
    Pages 2, 7, 8, 9, 14,
    21

3. VARIETAS
    Endpapers dated 1790, 1814.
    66 pages, 7¾ by 6½ inches, leatherbound.
    Pages headed: Extracts, Philosophy, Natural and Experimental,
    Natural History, Politics, Painting, Sketching, Dictionary
    of Natural History, Recipes. Copied texts; water-color sketches
    of animals, birds, insects, human eyes; some titled or
    annotated. Several pages blank.
    Jonathan Fisher Memorial.

4. NOTEBOOK
    Untitled, but many pages headed: Natural History.
    32 pages, 9⅜ by 7¼ inches, leatherbound.
    18 pages of water-color sketches of animals, birds, insects
    and butterflies, flowers, fruits, nuts, carrot; some
    with text; dated 1793, 1794, 1798, 1800, 1808, 1813, 1820,
    1821, 1826. The last 2 pages, floor plan of Fisher's 1814 house,
    in black ink, have been disbound and framed. Several pages blank.
    Jonathan Fisher Memorial.

Books illustrated with wood engravings by Fisher

1. THE YOUTH'S PRIMER, Containing a series of short verses in
    alphabetical order, each followed by religious, moral or
    historical observations. . . . Adorned with cuts. By Jonathan
    Fisher A.M. Boston, Samuel T. Armstrong, 1817; 1818.
    28 wood engravings by Fisher, most of them signed, some
    dated 1807 to 1812.

2. HYMNS FOR INFANT MINDS. Boston, Samuel T. Armstrong, 1819.
    14 wood engravings by Fisher, of which 8 are signed;
    frontispiece and cover cut probably not by him.

3. YOUTHFUL PIETY: A Memoir of Miriam Warner . . . and of Eliza
    M'Carty . . . Boston, Samuel T. Armstrong, 1820.
    2 wood engravings by Fisher, initialed; 3 by other hands.

4. SHORT POEMS: Including a Sketch of the Scriptures to the
    Book of Ruth . . . and a Few Others on Various Subjects.
    By Jonathan Fisher. Portland, A. Shirley, 1827.
    2 wood engravings by Fisher, 1 after John Collett after
    Hogarth, the other probably original.

5. SCRIPTURE ANIMALS, or Natural History of the Living Creatures
    Named in the Bible, Written Especially for Youth. Illustrated
    with Cuts. By Jonathan Fisher, A.M. Portland, William Hyde, 1834.
    142 wood engravings, including frontispiece. An unabridged
    republication of this book, with a foreword by Mary Ellen Chase,
    was issued by The Pyne Press, Princeton, New Jersey, in 1972.

6. DIVINE SONGS, Attempted in Easy Language for the Use of
    Children. Boston, Samuel T. Armstrong, 1819.
    8 wood engravings from Fisher's *Youth's Primer*.

7. ORIGINAL HYMNS FOR SABBATH SCHOOLS. Boston, Samuel T.
    Armstrong, 1820.
    1 wood engraving by Fisher; 4 illustrations plus frontispiece
    and cover cut probably not by him.

Sources and Credits

Pages 2, 3, photographs by Mark Sexton; page 15, courtesy Bangor Theological Seminary; plates 34, 35, 36, 37, 40, photographs by Mark Sexton; plate 38, photograph by Willard Starks; plate 39, photograph by Helga Studios. Woodcuts from *Scripture Animals* from a copy of the original imprint belonging to the Jonathan Fisher Memorial, Inc. All other illustrations reproduced from Jonathan Fisher's original notebooks in the possession of the Jonathan Fisher Memorial, Inc.